SHAKER ARCHITECTURE

Compiled by Herbert Schiffer

1469 Morstein Road, West Chester, Pennsylvania 19380

Jacket photographs courtesy Shaker Village at
Pleasant Hill, Kentucky, Inc. Front: Centre Family
Dwelling house. Back: East Family Brethren's
shop.

Printed in the United States of America.
ISBN: 0-88740-153-8
Published by Schiffer Publishing Ltd.
1469 Morstein Road, West Chester, Pennsylvania 19380

This book may be purchased from the publisher.
Please include $2.00 postage.
Try your bookstore first.

Acknowledgements

The following persons and their staffs are gratefully acknowledged for their cooperation throughout this project. Many questions were answered and many more arose, yet they each thought the problems through and found the answers. Sincere thanks are offered to each of you.

John Poppeliers, Chief, Historic American Buildings Survey. The illustrations are H.A.B.S. photographs except as noted, and much of the text has been extracted from H.A.B.S. reports. Mary Ison, Library of Congress, Prints and Photographs Section, Historic American Buildings Survey, for making her files completely available, guiding me through them, and being patient beyond belief. Edward Nickels, Director of Collection and Exhibits, Shakertown at Pleasant Hill, Kentucky. James Thomas, President, Pleasant Hill, Kentucky. Jane Brown, Coordinator of Communications, Pleasant Hill, Kentucky. Beatrice Taylor, Andrews Collection Librarian, Winterthur. Mrs. Neville Thompson, Manuscript Librarian, Winterthur. Margaret M. Nutt for organizing the material.

Foreword

Each chapter here presents a separate Shaker community. An attempt has been made to show as many types of buildings as possible. After showing a type of building in the early chapters, the type is not repeated without special reason in later chapters. Small, specialized buildings such as poultry houses are not shown separately because they are so similar to other multipurpose Shaker buildings as to be indistinguishable.

Details of history, religion, biography, and economic history enter this book only when they are directly relevant to the architecture of the Shakers.

Several Shaker communities have been restored and are open to the public. Hancock and Pleasant Hill are the two largest restorations and are definitely worth visiting. The communities at Canterbury, New Hampshire and New Gloucester, Maine still have active members, but upon their deaths the land and buildings will become museums.

Today, many Shaker buildings have been destroyed or altered for other purposes and others are being torn down at the time of this writing. At the same time, libraries, museums, and historic societies are being expanded to show their growing collections of Shaker objects. These groups seem to be working in opposition. Hopefully they can join to save the buildings.

Table of Contents

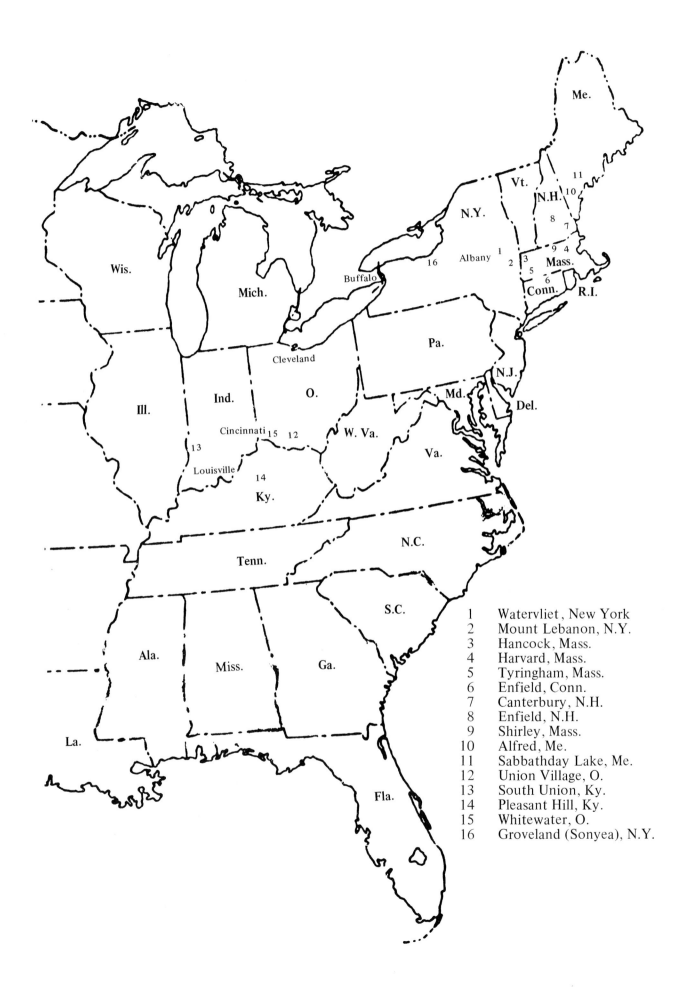

1   Watervliet, New York
2   Mount Lebanon, N.Y.
3   Hancock, Mass.
4   Harvard, Mass.
5   Tyringham, Mass.
6   Enfield, Conn.
7   Canterbury, N.H.
8   Enfield, N.H.
9   Shirley, Mass.
10 Alfred, Me.
11 Sabbathday Lake, Me.
12 Union Village, O.
13 South Union, Ky.
14 Pleasant Hill, Ky.
15 Whitewater, O.
16 Groveland (Sonyea), N.Y.

Introduction

THE SHAKER SOCIETY

Social and spiritual unrest in Europe during the eighteenth and nineteenth centuries brought thousands of people in search of a new way of life to the American shores. Among the newcomers were those who attempted to establish communities based on religious or socio-economic theories; few of these settlements survived. One of the most successful of the utopian experiments was begun in the swamplands of Niskeyuna near Albany, New York by the United Society of Believers in Christ's Second Appearing, under the leadership of Ann Lee (1736–1787), an illiterate textile worker from Manchester, England.

At the age of twenty-three, Ann Lees, (the 's' was later dropped), a blacksmith's daughter, joined the United Believers, a sect founded near Manchester by two dissident Quakers, James and Jane Wardley. The group derived many of its beliefs from the Quakers. The form of worship, involving the use of singing, shouting, and frenzied physical movement, was influenced by the French millennialists, known as the French Prophets or Camisards. The Believers were at first derisively referred to as Shaking Quakers, and then simply as Shakers. Many thought their doctrines smacked of "popery" and their strange manner of worship suggested witchcraft. Consequently, they were bitterly persecuted––physically abused and imprisoned.

Ann Lee married Abraham Standerin, a blacksmith, and their four children all died in infancy. In 1770, during one of her terms of incarceration for profaning the Sabbath, she experienced a vision in which it was revealed to her that "lustful gratifications of the flesh" were the "source and foundation of human corruption" and that only through the celibate life could man gain perfection. The concept of sexual abstinence had a substantial basis in the biblical story of Adam and Eve and in the belief held for so many centuries by the Church of Rome. Ann Lee's sad married life helped her accept this restriction.

As a result of Ann Lee's revelation, the Believers looked to her as the female representative of Christ on earth or their "Mother in Christ", and they thereafter adopted the rule of celibacy, leaving themselves open to further accusations of "popery".

Several years later, Ann Lee was instructed in another vision to take her followers to America. In May, 1774, she sailed from England on the *Mariah* with her husband (who left her soon afterward), John Hocknell, his son Richard, James Whittaker, a weaver, Mary Partington, James Shepherd, Ann Lee's niece Nancy Lees, and brother William Lees. They arrived in New York on August 6, and stayed there for two years working in their respective professions. Ann Lee worked as a laundress.

In 1775, John Hocknell, who financed the group's trip to America, leased a farm at Niskeyuna near Albany, New York. In the spring of 1776 the original group reunited there. For three years they concentrated on the work of creating a settlement in the wilderness and made little attempt to attract new followers.

In 1779, a revival––part of the eighteenth century religious movement known as the "Great Awakening"––took place among the New Light Baptists in nearby New Lebanon and the surrounding area. By the spring of the next year, word of the curious sect at Niskeyuna had reached the leaders of the revival; among them was the influential Preacher Joseph Meacham. Along with two companions, Meacham visited the Shakers and was converted on the day of his arrival. Soon thereafter, as Mother Ann had prophesied, others followed. People flocked to the settlement to hear Mother Ann and James Whittaker expound on the four basic Shaker beliefs: 1) the confession of sins, 2) the virtues of the celibate life, 3) the equality of the sexes, and 4) the consecration of labor. Between 1782 and 1784, Mother Ann and her disciples traveled throughout New England proselytizing and arousing antagonism among unbelievers wherever they went. They were accused by their enemies of destroying family life and spying for the British. It is ironic that while a war for political freedom raged around them they were denied the opportunity to express their own beliefs. As a result of the hostility they encountered, the new converts naturally drew together to practice their way of life and to provide mutual support against outsiders. By the time of Mother Ann's death in September of 1784, there were incipient communities of Shakers scattered throughout New England.

Ann Lee and William Lee both died soon after returning to Niskeyuna from their tour of New England. The leadership of the Society was transferred to James Whittaker. In protest over the selection of Whittaker, James Shepherd and John Partington left the Society, and Richard Hocknell and Nancy Lees left and were married. When James Whittaker died three years later in 1787, the Preacher–convert Joseph Meacham was chosen to become spiritual leader. He chose Lucy Wright to lead the women.

Since most of the new converts were poor farmers and artisans, they were required to pool their resources to survive. Accordingly, stringent rules regarding communal property evolved, as well as a hierarchy of leaders called the "ministry" to direct and coordinate the individual communities. It is thought that James Whittaker was the first to enunciate the rule of common property, but it was under his successor, Joseph Meacham, that this rule was clarified and given structure.

Although the Shakers maintained a celibate life and separation of the sexes, it was not the complete separation that is observed in monasteries or convents. The Shakers chose instead to create "families" in which the brethren and sisters

lived, worshiped, and worked together on equal terms, and to a limited extent even socialized with one another. As the community plan evolved, the first "family" was usually called the Church or Centre Family and the others were named as they related to it chronologically or geographically, as the Second Family or the South Family. Each "family" usually maintained its own dwelling and service buildings, such as a laundry, a barn, and various workshops. Some structures, such as the meetinghouse, the school, and usually the trustees' office, where business was transacted with the outside world, were used by the whole community, and these were ordinarily located in the Church Family.

Each family in a Society was governed by a system of Elders and Eldresses, Deacons and Deaconesses, and male and female Trustees. Two Elders and two Eldresses, of equal status, were responsible for the spiritual affairs of the members of each family.

The family was an independent economic order whose temporal affairs were managed by the Deacons and Trustees. The Deacons were in charge of the industrial activities. The Trustees were in charge of the finances.

As the number of conversions to the Shaker faith increased, it seemed most practical to form communities where the faithful could worship and practice their way of life free from persecution. To that end, in 1787, Joseph Meacham sent word from Niskeyuna to the scattered faithful in New York and the New England states that

SEPTEMBER 13, 1873.]   FRANK LESLIE'S ILLUSTRATED NEWSPAPER.   13

THE DINING-ROOM OF THE NORTH FAMILY.

New York State Library Collection

This is from a sketch from Frank Leslie's Monthly in 1885.

those who were prepared should gather at New Lebanon, New York, in the hill country near the Massachusetts border. Here a group of believers had already donated land and built a meetinghouse for this purpose. Although not the first Shaker community founded, New Lebanon, or Mount Lebanon, as it was renamed after 1861, was the first to be formally "gathered into society order", and it became the governing or parent society for all the other villages. The community plan and the architectural forms created out of necessity at Mount Lebanon were used as models by all subsequently established societies. For example, the meetinghouse designed by the architect Moses Johnson in 1787 was duplicated under his direction in most of the other New England communities. Therefore, the Editor has selected a large number of pictures for this volume from the Watervliet and Mount Lebanon communities, as until the community at Pleasant Hill, Kentucky was built, few buildings were not strongly influenced by ideas and workmen from Mount Lebanon.

Confusion has arisen in the records of early Shaker settlements between the date of the founding and the 'gathering' of the different communities. The date of founding was somewhat indefinite, since it might mean only the meeting together of two or three converts. Usually these early Believers worshiped in private houses or even out of doors, and the members continued living with their own 'natural' families. 'Gathering', however, or 'gathering into gospel order', meant joining together in communal living. It also included the signing of a covenant. None of the societies were 'gathered' in this sense until 1787, but a good many were founded in the four years of Mother Ann's ministry between 1780 and 1784.[1]

In 1796, Joseph Meacham died and Mother Lucy Wright became leader of the central ministry at Mount Lebanon.

In 1805 Mother Lucy sent missionaries to Kentucky. With Father Joseph, she had formulated the precepts which were later set down as statutes and ordinances of the Millennial Laws. These Laws were issued in 1821 and revised in 1845, 1860, 1887, and most recently in 1938. In 1821 when Mother Lucy died, the Shaker Society was growing rapidly and developing into a cohesive movement. Between 1787 and 1826, nineteen Shaker colonies in seven states were formed and directed from the central ministry at Mount Lebanon. These included twelve communities in New England, four in Ohio, two in Kentucky, and one in Indiana. At first, agriculture was the foundation of the Shaker economy, but as time progressed manufacturing became more important, particularly in the northern societies. At the apex of their development in the decade before the Civil War, there were as many as 6,000 Shakers living in self-sufficient communities in varying degrees of prosperity. After the Civil War, however, membership in the United Society began to fall off precipitously. The reasons for the decline were complex and are still debated. Explanations that recur most frequently suggest that material well-being, once achieved, undermined the original ardor. As a religious system Shakerism had a strong justification and appeal, but as a socio-economic system it could not compete with the "world".

The adoption and raising of orphaned children developed among the Shakers as a necessity for survival of their celibate society. As long as these children and regular converts were joining the communities, labor was available. Since until the American Civil War there were few agencies able to cope with children available for adoption, and few jobs were open to widows and young women, the Shakers were able to grow in numbers quite easily by tending to orphans. These orphaned children stayed with the Shakers until they were twenty-one. Then they were given the choice of joining the group or leaving. These children were given good educations for which they did a great deal of work.

Shaker buildings were placed in relation to one another with fitness and efficiency in mind, presenting a pleasing and well ordered community plan. The principle structures were usually located around an inner court or yard and along a main access road, the shops behind, and a large barn sprawling off at a distance. The Shakers were obviously aware that their spotless, peaceful little villages were a means of gaining respect among their neighbors and attracting new believers to their way of life. Their gardens and fields were carefully manicured, their buildings and fences freshly painted, and their streets generously planted with trees.

[1]Marguerite Fellows Melcher, *The Shaker Adventure,* (Cleveland: Western Reserve University Press, 1941), p. 34-5.

Building forms were dictated by the needs of the community. The functional patterns established at Mount Lebanon were repeated at all subsequently founded communities. This is not to imply that they all appeared to be stamped out of the same mold, for each was a variation on a theme, with little differences influenced by the time of the community's founding, the geographic location, and materials available, as well as the ability of the builders. These communities which now seem in some respects models of modern planning——including such concepts as the clustering of dwellings and service buildings in small groups to locate the proper balance of activity and privacy and to the optimum use of the surrounding land——evolved as a result of the Shaker demand for order and efficiency. Far from being the products of sophisticated schools of architecture and environmental design, Shaker builders and planners had little or no training.

In most cases the architect is not known, or there is no architect, as the buildings were actually community efforts. There are no plans to study, no written record of the construction, and information is very sparse about buildings which have been torn down. With the exception of the young carpenters, Micajah Burnett (1791–1879) of Pleasant Hill, Kentucky and Moses Johnson (1752–1842) of Enfield, New Hampshire, architects' names are forgotten. The latter probably had the greatest influence on Shaker community design; his name is generally associated with the gambrel-roofed meetinghouses he built throughout New England, but he was also responsible for the design and construction of many other buildings, including shops, mills, and even a hogsty at Watervliet, New York.

Moses Johnson was born in 1752 and lived near Enfield, New Hampshire in 1782, when Shakers came to that area to make converts. In October of that year, Moses Johnson, his wife and three children entered the Society. He must have been an experienced carpenter then, for in 1785 he was given the job of framing and supervising construction of the church at Mount Lebanon, New York, over two hundred miles away. With that building done, he moved to Hancock, Massachusetts to supervise the meetinghouse built there in 1786. By then, his style seems to have been solidified and his work was in demand. In the next years, he supervised the meetinghouses at Watervliet, in 1791; Enfield, Connecticut in 1791; Harvard, Massachusetts in 1792; Canterbury, New Hampshire in 1792; Shirley, Massachusetts in 1793; Enfield, New Hampshire in 1793; Alfred, Maine in 1793; and Sabbathday Lake, Maine in 1793.

The meetinghouse, as the focal point of the Society, was among the first buildings to be raised. Not unexpectedly, most did not differ greatly from the vernacular style of the rural architecture of the surrounding countryside. They typically were rectangular with two entrances at one end for the clergy, both men and women. Separate entrances for the male (brethren) and female members (sisters) were on the long side of the building. The interior was built without visible supports since the meetings included a round

The world's people were invited to watch spiritual exercises. Note the figure in the lower left.

dance for which posts would be a hindrance. To obtain the open floor space, an arched truss was built to support the roof, and this has come to be known as a "rainbow roof". The interior usually had a stepped gallery at one end for visitors, while the Shakers sat men on one end and women opposite on moveable benches, which were moved to the sides before the dancing began. The second floor was divided into residence and office rooms for the Elders.

There was little ornamentation. By the time the Millennial Laws were written formally in 1821, it was traditional that the exterior of meeting-houses be white, with blue interior trim, and yellow or red painted floors. Two rows of pegs decorated the walls and held coats and hats. Otherwise, the walls were plain.

The Millennial Law includes the following ten points concerning building, painting, varnishing and the manufacture of articles for sale:

1. Beadings, mouldings and cornices, which are merely for fancy may not be made by Believers.

2. Odd or fanciful styles of architecture, may not be used among Believers, neither should any deviate widely from the common styles of building among Believers, without the union of the Ministry.

3. The meeting house should be painted white without, and of a blueish shade within. Houses and shops, should be as near uniform in color, as consistent; but it is advisable to have shops of a little darker shade than dwelling houses.

4. Floors in dwelling houses, if stained at all, should be of a reddish yellow, and shop floors should be of a yellowish red.

5. It is unadvisable for wooden buildings, fronting the street, to be painted red, brown, or black, but they should be of a lightish hue.

6. No buildings may be painted white, save meeting houses.

7. Barns and back buildings, as wood houses, etc. if painted at all, should be of a dark hue, either red, or brown, lead color, or something of the kind, unless they front the road, or command a sightly aspect, and then they should not be of a very light color.

8. It is considered imprudent and is therefore not allowable, to paint or oil such articles as the following, viz. Cart and ox waggon bodies, or any kind of lumber waggon or sleigh boxes, sleds or sleighs, except those kept at the office for journeying; wheelbarrows, and hand cart bodies, or hand sleds for rough use, hoe handles, or fork stales, rake stales, broom or mop handles, for home use, plough beams, milking stools, and all such articles as are exposed to very ready wear, whether for in doors or out.

9. The following articles may be painted, viz. All kinds of cart and waggon wheels and gearing. All kinds of carriages and sleighs for nice use, wheelbarrows, hand carts, and hand sleds, kept exclusively for nice use. Ox yokes and snow shovels, may be stained or oiled. The frames of cart and waggon bodies, also gates may be put together with paint,[2] but not painted.

10. Varnish, if used in dwelling houses, may be applied only to the moveables therein, as the following, viz. Tables, stands, bureaus, cases of drawers, writing desks, or boxes, drawer faces, chests, chairs, etc. etc. Carriages kept exclusively for riding or nice use may be varnished. No ceilings, casings or mouldings, may be varnished. Oval or nice boxes may be stained reddish or yellow, but not varnished. Bannisters or hand rails in dwelling houses may be varnished.[3]

Because of the law of celibacy and the size of the Shaker "families" that had to be housed under one roof, the dwelling house presented the most interesting design problem. The solution was a dormitory-like structure separated within by dual hallways and stairways, and without by dual entrances. There were also dwelling houses designed specifically for children, as the Shakers often brought their own offspring with them when they joined the Society, and the Society made it a practice for many years to take in orphans. The spacious interiors of these buildings were in perfect keeping with the exteriors—spare, well-proportioned rooms, perfectly maintained in accordance with every detail prescribed by the Millennial Laws.

[2]To resist rust.—Ed.

[3]Section IX of *The Millennial Law* as transcribed in Edward Deming Andrews' book, *The People Called Shakers*, pp. 285-286.

Pleasant Hill Centre Family Dwelling House. Front hall, second floor, looking north.

Hancock Church Family Main Dwelling House. Clothes peg board detail.

At the Pleasant Hill, Kentucky community, Micajah Burnett is responsible for most of the important buildings. Micajah Burnett was born in Virginia in 1791. Little is known of his life, but it is certain that he did not have formal training in architecture, yet he was fondly remembered as the master carpenter, architect, and town planner of Pleasant Hill. In 1813 he revised the orientation of the village by changing the important axis from north-south to east-west. During 1817 he supervised the building of the East Family House. The meetinghouse was next in 1820. The largest of his buildings was the Centre Family House of 1824. In 1833 he supervised construction of the water system at Pleasant Hill which was the first public water works west of the Allegheny Mountains. In 1839 he constructed the Trustees' House. Besides his role as architect, he became the trading Deacon here and traveled extensively selling Shaker products and recruiting orphaned children.

Barns were essential to these agriculture-based communities, and the Shakers built very large ones, often incorporating their own innovations. They were built of stone and/or wood depending on locale, and often designed into a hillside to provide for unloading on all levels. The upper floors were for hay and grain storage while the livestock was kept below. The barn of the North Family at Mount Lebanon had a tremendous manure pit filled by a system of buckets which ran on a semi-circular catwalk on the cows' level and emptied at the level below.

The economic structure of the communities dictated the need for small, specialized buildings of many types. Those connected with the farms are standard: for livestock, hay, grain, and equipment storage. The Brethren and Sisters might have a separate building each for their trades such as making brooms and furniture, weaving, laundry, seed sorting and packaging. Examples are shown both as separate buildings and as parts of larger structures adapted for particular use.

Hancock Church Family Washhouse and Machine Shop. Laundry room.

Hancock Church Family Washhouse and Machine Shop. Ironing room.

The Shakers' early industrial techniques were ahead of their time; such as having sewing rooms facing south and west for maximum light, and placing laundry rooms on the ground floor so that heavy wet loads of wash could be put on the clothes lines without being carried upstairs from a basement. The Shakers have been given credit for inventing the washing machine.

The Seed industry was so large that in one year before the War, 79,000 papers of seeds and 17,000 jars of preserves and jellies were made and sold. This tool is a seed gathering tool for gathering Kentucky blue grass seed.

Church Family Sisters' Shop (first). Workroom.

One of the Shakers' most important industries was basket weaving. Indians have been given credit for teaching Shakers basketry, herb law and dyeing. In the basket shop of the Mount Lebanon community, at least 76 types of baskets were made, from 3" sewing baskets to split black ash baskets for storing barks, roots and herbs, and were six feet long. In 1842 a visitor said, "This Sect's baskets are unsurpassed in quality."

At New Lebanon, in 1828, the Brothers Amos Bisby and Henry Bennett invented the tongue and groove machine.

Extensive travels of Elders of each community to sell the Shakers' products reflect the size and organization of their industries. So many crop seeds were sold nationally that an industry developed to print the labels and make boxes for them. Their attempt to be self-sufficient led the Shakers to have food-producing farms, leather tanneries, leather book binding facilities, and cobblers.

There is evidence that the Shakers invented:

    clothes pins
    therapeutic static electric machine
    water powered cooling fan
    chair tilters
    side hill plow
    sash weights
    Babbitt metal
    machines used for packing herbs
    cut nails
    circular saw
    screw propellers
    rotary harrows
    condensed milk
    pea shellers
    threshing machines
    silk reeling machines
and greatly improved:
    windmills
    fertilizer spreaders
    bed rollers
    screw-fed lathes
    lumber drying kilns

No matter how self-sufficient these people desired to be, they found themselves often in a position that demanded an involvement with the "world". The Main Dwelling of the Watervliet South Family with the exterior "call bell" at the gable ridge (characteristic of the main dwelling houses at all Shaker communities), was built by "Bruster and Allen, Master Masons" in 1822; however, the Shaker brethren did much of the labor and are responsible for all of the exterior woodwork. In details such as the third floor built-in drawers of pine and in the fitted corner cabinet at the rear of the first floor, the simplicity, yet fineness, of Shaker craftsmanship is shown.

There were several small groups of Shakers throughout the northeast United States which did not develop into communities such as those pictured in this book. Notable was a group of black Shakers in Philadelphia, a small group in Georgia and in Florida. There are no buildings built for or exclusively associated with these groups, so they are not emphasized here.

Hancock Church Family Brethren's Shop. East portion of first floor, showing heating stove.

Shaker stoves varied greatly according to a study of two hundred examples. There were, however, two similar characteristics: one, the doors opened left to right; the other, the simplicity of design, and in most cases they were cast in less pieces than other stoves. One of the greatest variables is the legs - most are of cast iron, while some are wrought iron with penny feet, or cabriole shape.

Jack E. Boucher, Photographer

James Irving, Photographer

This is a group of vigorous Shakers in the 1860's, at the height of the Shaker influence and prosperity. They pose here at the Great Gate at the Watervliet community. (Courtesy, Henry Francis duPont Winterthur Museum Libraries, The Edward Deming Andrews Memorial Shaker Collection, No. SA158.)

Chapter 1
Watervliet, New York

(Niskeyuna)

1787–1938

Location: North of intersection of Troy Shaker Road (State route 155) and Albany Shaker Road, Albany County, New York.

This was the first American Shaker community, dating from 1775 when John Hocknell leased 200 acres of land. (At that time the area was known as Niskeyuna). Ann Lee and her eight original followers gathered here after being dispersed for two years following their arrival in New York from England.

The community grew rapidly after the first conversions in 1779 which included that of Joseph Meacham. Meacham was formerly a preacher of the New Light Baptists at New Lebanon, New York. His stature among the Shakers grew rapidly until 1787 when he was chosen to be the spiritual leader of the community. Under his leadership the Shakers became thoroughly organized and the structures of the communal society came into being.

The buildings at Watervliet were built gradually as the community grew. David Austin Buckingham, Shaker and historian of the Watervliet Church Family, listed in an 1825 report that the first dwelling house was built "....in 1778, a second house in 1783, an addition to the first dwelling house in 1784, and the 'Old log meeting house' in 1784." [4]

The Watervliet community grew in population steadily until its peak between 1825 and 1850 to about 350 members. Their industries flourished and many inventions were made here. At Watervliet bonnets, fine shirts, and flat brooms were made and sold to the world. A garden seed business had a modest beginning at Watervliet in the 1790's and gradually increased to a very significant size. As the industries and populations grew, new buildings were constructed for specific needs.

The population declined during the Civil War period and never again recovered, yet financially the community was sound and growing wealthier. Real estate was purchased by the community and kept in perfect order by committees within each family. When the Shakers' numbers were dwindling, hired workers were obtained to maintain the properties.

Many serious fires plagued the Watervliet community over the years and gradually destroyed many of the buildings. Thirteen buildings of the North Family settlement burned on April 15, 1927, and a fire there in 1932 destroyed the remaining buildings.

The Watervliet community closed on July 18, 1938 after the death of Eldress Anna Case.

Author Herman Melville lived in Albany from 1830–1838 and wrote some of his first books in Lansingburgh, north of Troy, and must have had first-hand knowledge of the Watervliet (Niskeyuna) Shakers. In *Moby Dick* he tells of a member of the crew of the *Jeroboam* having been "nurtured among the crazy society of the Neskeuna Shakers, where he had been a great prophet; in their cracked, secret meetings, having several times descended from heaven by the way of a trap-door." [5]

[4] D.A. Buckingham. "List of Decayed Buildings", (Cleveland: Western Reserve Historical Society, c. 1825.)

[5] Herman Melville. *Moby Dick: or The Whale* (Rhinehart, 1948), p. 311.

Church Family. General view of inner "yard" looking north c. 1920's.

Church Family. General view of inner "yard" looking north.

William F. Winter, Jr., Photographer

Church Family. General view of inner "yard" looking south.

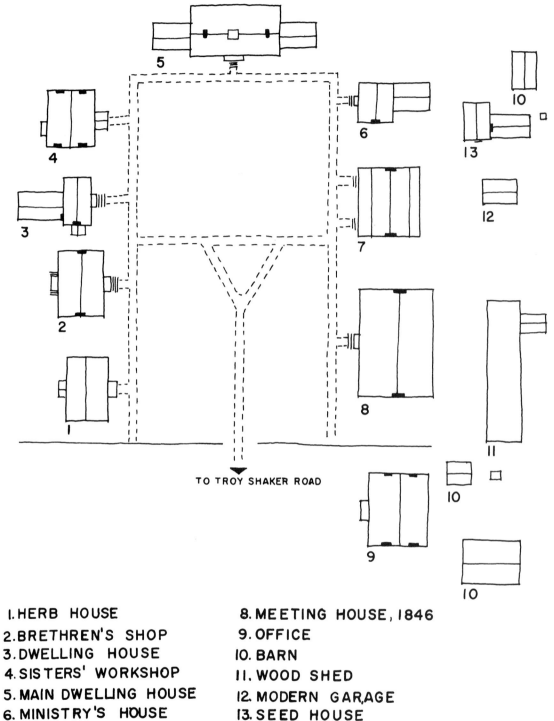

TO TROY SHAKER ROAD

1. HERB HOUSE
2. BRETHREN'S SHOP
3. DWELLING HOUSE
4. SISTERS' WORKSHOP
5. MAIN DWELLING HOUSE
6. MINISTRY'S HOUSE
7. MEETING HOUSE, 1791

8. MEETING HOUSE, 1846
9. OFFICE
10. BARN
11. WOOD SHED
12. MODERN GARAGE
13. SEED HOUSE

Sketch plan of Watervliet Shakers Church Family

E. J. Stein, Photographer

Church Family. New Meetinghouse. View from northwest. The new meetinghouse was of frame construction measuring 113 feet by 54 feet. Sister Ann Buckingham, a member of this community, wrote in her diary on June 27, 1847, "Raise new meeting house. Oliver Prentice's boys, all the Brethren in the society that could do as much as pull a rope, came to the raising." (New York State History Collection)

William F. Winter, Jr., Photographer

Church Family. New Meetinghouse. North elevation.

Church Family. New Meetinghouse. South end of meeting room.

E. J. Stein, Photographer

William F. Winter, Jr., Photographer

Church Family. New Meetinghouse. Northwest corner of meeting room.

E. J. Stein, Photographer

Church Family. Sisters' Workshop. View from southeast.

E. J. Stein, Photographer

Church Family. Sisters' Workshop.
Basement door, west (rear) elevation.

William F. Winter, Jr., Photographer

Church Family. Brethren's Workshop. View from southwest.

William F. Winter, Jr., Photographer

Church Family. Laundry and Canning Factory. South and west elevations.

E. J. Stein, Photographer

Church Family. Herb House. View from southeast.

William F. Winter, Jr., Photographer

E. J. Stein, Photographer

Church Family. Herb House. View from northwest.

Church Family. Herb House. Interior view with herb press.

Church Family Seed House. View from southwest.

E. J. Stein, Photographer

E. J. Stein, Photographer

Church Family. Main dwelling house. South elevation.

E. J. Stein, Photographer

Church Family Mill. General view.

North Family. General view looking south.   Probably 1920's.

North Family dwelling house. General view.

North Family old second house. General view.   Note the two elderly Shakers.

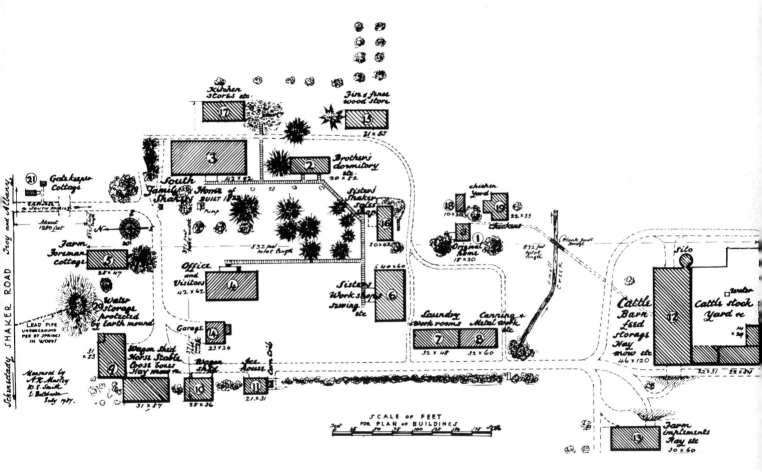

Group plan of buildings of the South Family of Shakers

N. E. Baldwin, Photographer

South Family. General view from barn.

N. E. Baldwin, Photographer

South Family. General view showing small barn and Superintendent's house.

N. E. Baldwin, Photographer

South Family residence, building #3. West (main) elevation.

N. E. Baldwin, Photographer

South Family residence, building #3. Arch kettle in kitchen.

N. E. Baldwin, Photographer

South Family Brothers' Workshop, building #4. West and south sides

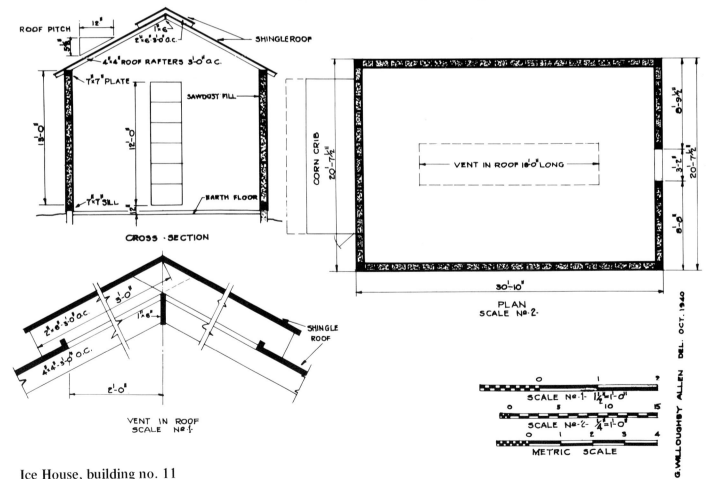

Ice House, building no. 11

South Family woodshed, building #15. Exterior from west.

South Family woodshed, building #15. Interior.

South Family Ash House. Ashes were the basis of lye used in soap.

South Family cow and hay barn, building # 12. From northeast.

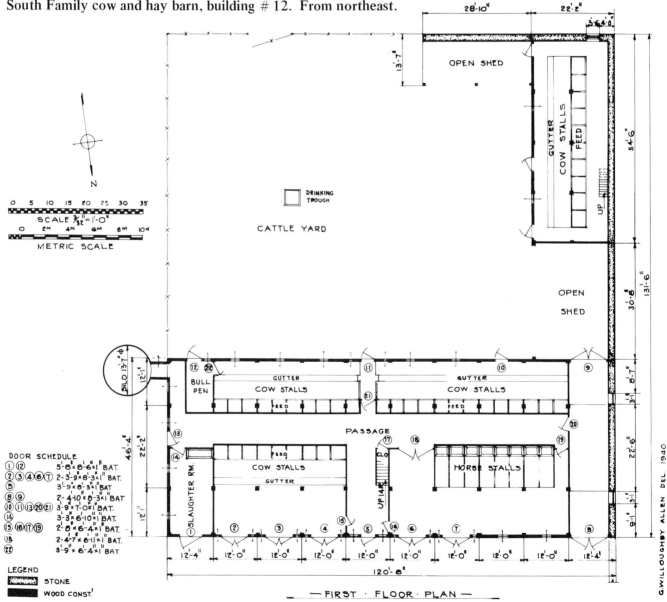

28'-10" 22'-2"

36'-0"

13'-7"

OPEN SHED

OPEN SHED

GUTTER

COW STALLS

FEED

UP

54'-6"

30'-8" 13'-6"

DRINKING TROUGH

CATTLE YARD

N

0 5 10 15 20 25 30 35

SCALE 3/32" = 1'-0"

0 2M 4M 6M 8M 10M

METRIC SCALE

SILO 13'-7" Ø

12'-1"

12 22

BULL PEN

GUTTER

COW STALLS

FEED

11

21

GUTTER

COW STALLS

FEED

10

9

8'-7"

3'-1"

22'-6"

PASSAGE

17 18

CLO.

UP 14'-6"

19

20

13

14

SLAUGHTER RM.

COW STALLS

GUTTER

FEED

HORSE STALLS

15 16 17 19

46'-4" 22'-2"

12'-1"

DOOR SCHEDULE

1 12   5'-8" x 8'-6" x 1" BAT.
2 3 4 6 7   2'-3.9" x 8'-3" x 1" BAT.
5   3'-9" x 8'-3" x 1" BAT.
8 9   2'-4.10" x 8'-3" x 1" BAT.
10 11 13 20 21   3'-9" x 7'-0" x 1" BAT.
14   3'-3" x 6'-10" x 1" BAT.
15 16 17 19   2'-8" x 6'-4" x 1" BAT.
18   2'-4.7" x 6'-11" x 1" BAT.
22   3'-9" x 6'-4" x 1" BAT.

1 2 3 4 15 5 18 6 7 8

12'-4" 12'-0" 12'-0" 12'-0" 12'-0" 12'-0" 12'-0" 12'-0" 12'-0" 12'-4"

120'-0"

LEGEND

STONE

WOOD CONST.

— FIRST · FLOOR · PLAN —

N. E. Baldwin, Photographer

West Family. General view from south.

West Family. General view.

West Family main dwelling, building #1. West (front) elevation.

N. E. Baldwin, Photographer

West Family main dwelling, building #1. Interior: with clothes press door, chimney closets and chimney clean-out, and built-in chest of drawers.

N. E. Baldwin, Photographer

West Family main dwelling, building #1. Attic - built-in drawers.

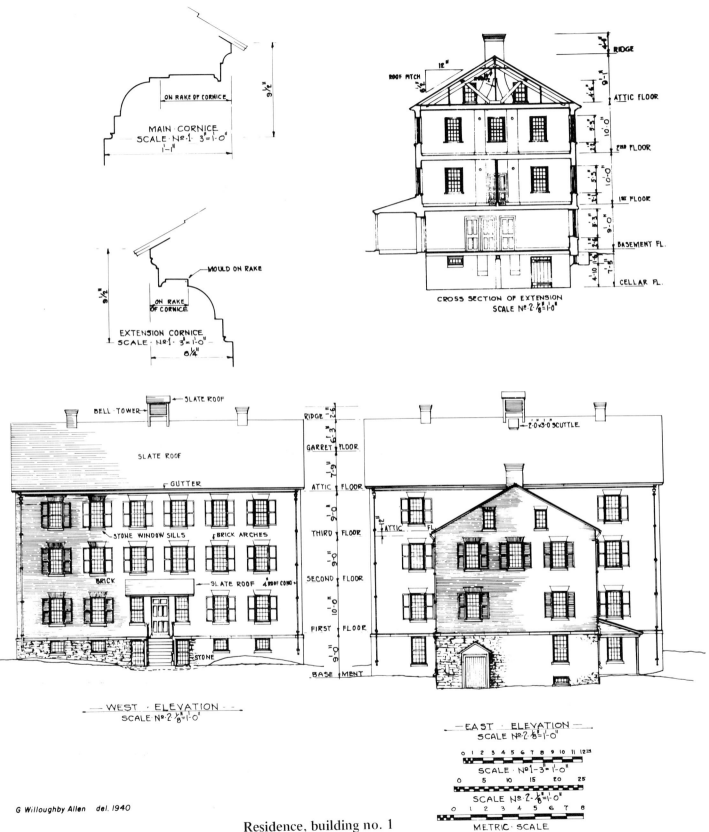

ON RAKE OF CORNICE

MAIN·CORNICE
SCALE·Nº·1· 3"=1'-0"
1-1"

MOULD ON RAKE

ON RAKE
OF CORNICE

EXTENSION CORNICE
SCALE·Nº·1· 3"=1'-0"
8¼"

CROSS SECTION OF EXTENSION
SCALE Nº 2· ⅛"=1'-0"

ROOF PITCH   12"
RIDGE
ATTIC FLOOR
2ND FLOOR
1ST FLOOR
BASEMENT FL.
CELLAR FL.

BELL·TOWER   SLATE ROOF
SLATE ROOF
GUTTER
STONE WINDOW SILLS   BRICK ARCHES
BRICK
SLATE ROOF   4"ROOF COND
STONE

RIDGE
GARRET FLOOR
ATTIC FLOOR
THIRD FLOOR
SECOND FLOOR
FIRST FLOOR
BASEMENT

2-0"x3-0" SCUTTLE
ATTIC FL

WEST·ELEVATION
SCALE Nº 2· ⅛"=1'-0"

EAST·ELEVATION
SCALE Nº 2· ⅛"=1'-0"

SCALE·Nº·1-3'=1'-0"

SCALE Nº 2·⅛"=1'-0"

METRIC·SCALE

G Willoughby Allen   del. 1940

Residence, building no. 1

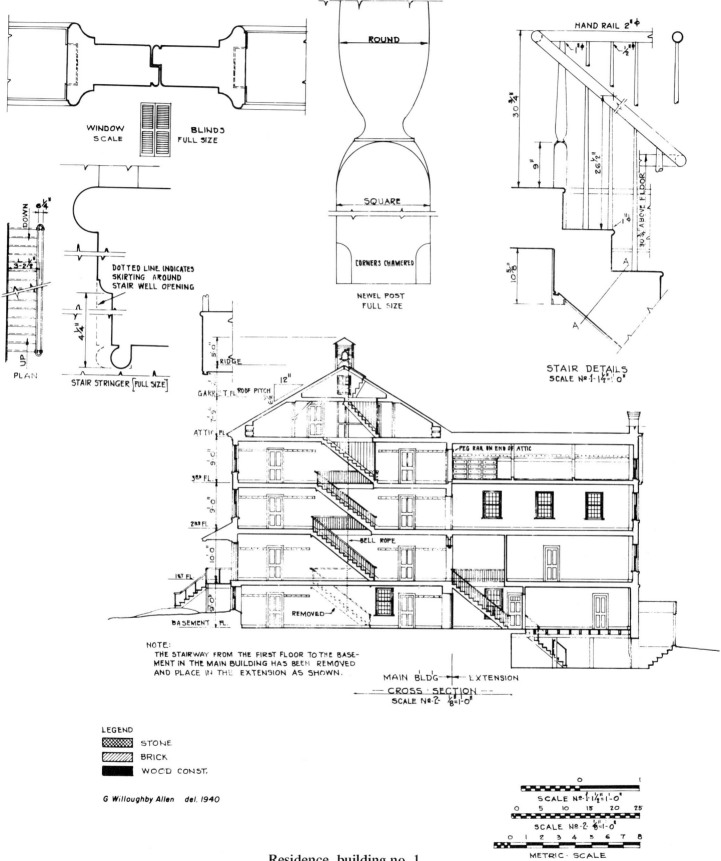

WINDOW
SCALE

BLINDS
FULL SIZE

ROUND

SQUARE

CORNERS CHAMFERED

NEWEL POST
FULL SIZE

HAND RAIL 2" φ

30 ¾"

9"

2'-6½"

30 ¾ ABOVE FLOOR

10 ⅝"

A

A

STAIR DETAILS
SCALE Nº 1- 1½"=1'-0"

DOWN

6¼"

3'-2¼"

UP

PLAN

DOTTED LINE INDICATES
SKIRTING AROUND
STAIR WELL OPENING

4'4"

STAIR STRINGER [FULL SIZE]

5'-0"

RIDGE

GARRET FL. ROOF PITCH

12"

ATTIC FL.

3RD FL.

2ND FL.

PEG RAIL ON END OF ATTIC

BELL ROPE

1ST FL.

REMOVED

BASEMENT FL.

NOTE:
THE STAIRWAY FROM THE FIRST FLOOR TO THE BASE-
MENT IN THE MAIN BUILDING HAS BEEN REMOVED
AND PLACE IN THE EXTENSION AS SHOWN.

MAIN BLDG — EXTENSION

CROSS SECTION
SCALE Nº 2- ⅛"=1'-0"

LEGEND
STONE
BRICK
WOOD CONST.

G Willoughby Allen   del. 1940

SCALE Nº 1- 1½"=1'-0"
0   5   10   15   20   25
SCALE Nº 2- ⅛"=1'-0"
0 1 2 3 4 5 6 7 8
METRIC SCALE

Residence, building no. 1

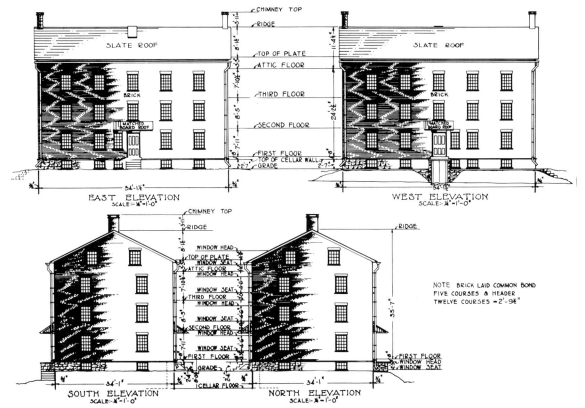

Workshop, building no. 3

Workshop, building no. 3

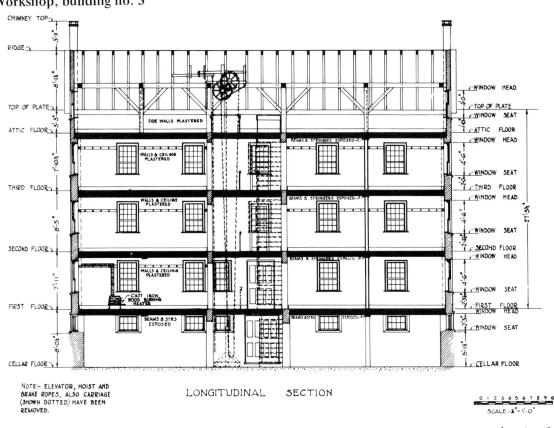

LONGITUDINAL   SECTION

NOTE:- ELEVATOR, HOIST AND
BRAKE ROPES, ALSO CARRIAGE
(SHOWN DOTTED) HAVE BEEN
REMOVED.

Chapter 2
Mount Lebanon, New York

(New Lebanon)
(1787–1947)

Location: Just west of New York-Massachusetts State line, approximately 1 mile southeast of New Lebanon and junction of State Route 22 and U.S. Route 20, on Shaker Road.

In the summer of 1779 a religious revival broke out in the area of New Lebanon and nearby Hancock, Massachusetts. A number of meetings were held on the property of a prosperous farmer, George Darrow, who eventually donated the land that became the center of the New Lebanon Shaker community. "The revival lasted all summer. All sorts of people attended the meetings: young, old, middle-aged; Methodists, Presbyterians, Baptists; men and women from poor and ignorant families, college graduates. The whole district was like one great revival meeting." [6] Yet, when the summer began to change into autumn and then into winter, few were able to retain the ardor and hope that had been the blessing of the warm summer months. The meetings disbanded, and two of the disillusioned, who set about in March of the next year (1780) evidently to find other "promised lands" further west, by chance stopped at Mother Ann's community of Niskeyuna (later called the Watervliet community). Impressed by the sincerity of Mother Ann and her small group of followers and by the physical manifestations of their spiritual life that in many ways resemble those of the recent revivals, they returned to inform the few leaders at New Lebanon, who had retained the fervor of the summer meetings, of this sect that in so many ways promised to fulfill their hopes and aspirations. Around this core the Shaker movement at New Lebanon began to grow.

The Shakers at New Lebanon were perhaps the most active of the Shaker communities by the late 1780's. With the lands and buildings donated, and with the goods — in most cases rather limited — of many others who embraced this belief, the physical hardships of the first few years were gradually overcome. Already on October 15, 1785 the first meetinghouse was raised. It was a plain, gambrel-roofed structure that was destined to become the typical meetinghouse type until 1805. Despite the simplicity and general use of this style of architecture in New England and New York, the building became "nevertheless the symbol of a faith established, the beginning of the church as 'an outward visible order.'" [7]

Charles Dickens' account of his visit to the Shakers at Mount Lebanon, New York, in 1842:

"We walked into a grim room, where several grim hats were hanging on grim pegs, and the time was grimly told by a grim clock....."

[6]Marguerite Fellows Melcher. *The Shaker Adventure* (Cleveland: Western Reserve University Press, 1941), p. 20.

[7]Edward Deming Andrews. *The People Called Shakers* (New York: Oxford University Press, 1953), p. 51.

New York — the Shakers at Lebanon

The Singing Meeting—from a sketch by Joseph Becker.

William F. Winter, Jr., Photographer

Church Family. General view from west.

N. E. Baldwin, Photographer

Church Family, main dwelling, building #1.
Front (east) elevation.

Church Family, main dwelling, building #1. Dining hall.

N. E. Baldwin, Photographer

The kitchen of the Church Family.

Church Family Meetinghouse, building #2. View from southwest.

William F. Winter, Jr., Photographer

Church Family Meetinghouse, building # 2. North side.

N.E. Baldwin, Photographer

Church Family Meetinghouse, building # 2. View to north of meeting room.

William F. Winter, Jr., Photographer

Church Family Meetinghouse, building # 2. View of visitors' gallery in meeting room.

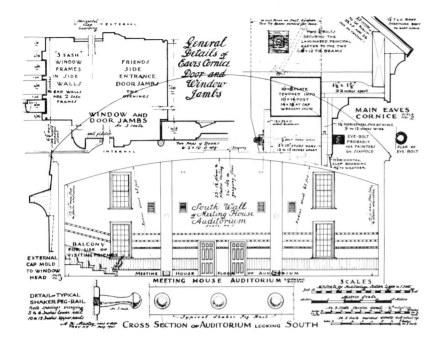

Church Family Meetinghouse, building #2. Meeting room - interior.

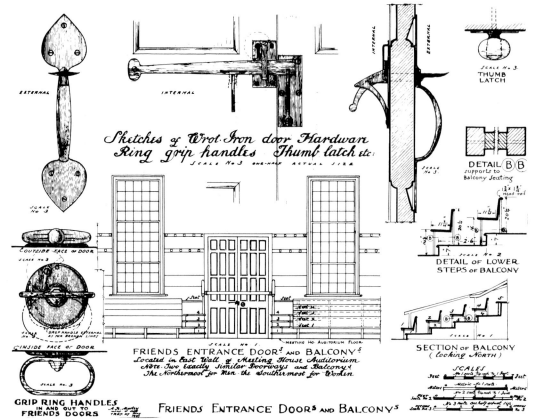

Meetinghouse Building No. 2

Church Family Brethren's Workshop, building # 3. Exterior view from west.

Church Family Brethren's Workshop, building # 3. Interior view of carpenters' shop. William F. Winter, Jr., Photographer

Photocopy of Lossing-Barritt engraving, circa 1875

Church Family Seed House (original meetinghouse).   Building # 4.

Church Family Tannery, building #9. View from southeast.

Church Family Infirmary, building #13. View from west (Sisters' Workshop in rear).

William F. Winter, Jr., Photographer

William F. Winter, Jr., Photographer

Church Family Infirmary, building #13. Detail of west elevation entry and canopy.

William F. Winter, Jr., Photographer

Church Family Sisters' Workshop, building #18.

Church Family school building - Front (west) elevation.

William F. Winter, Jr., Photographer

William F. Winter, Jr., Photographer

Church Family Sisters' Workshop, building #18.

Church Family school building - Front (west) elevation.

Jack Boucher, Photographer

Church Family apple drying kiln. Exterior view of kiln.

North Family. General view from west.

N. E. Baldwin, Photographer

North Family. General view from south.

N. E. Baldwin, Photographer

North Family residence, building # 1. East (front) side.

William F. Winter, Jr., Photographer

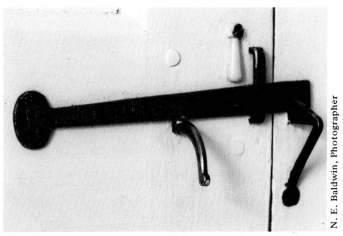

N. E. Baldwin, Photographer

North Family residence, building # 1. Interior door latch.

N. E. Baldwin, Photographer

North Family residence, building # 1.

N. E. Baldwin, Photographer

North Family residence, building # 1. Dining room door latch.

William F. Winter, Jr., Photographer

North Family residence, building #1. West and north sides.

N. E. Baldwin, Photographer

North Family residence, building #1. Canning kitchen. Elevator.

N. E. Baldwin, Photographer

North Family residence, building #1.

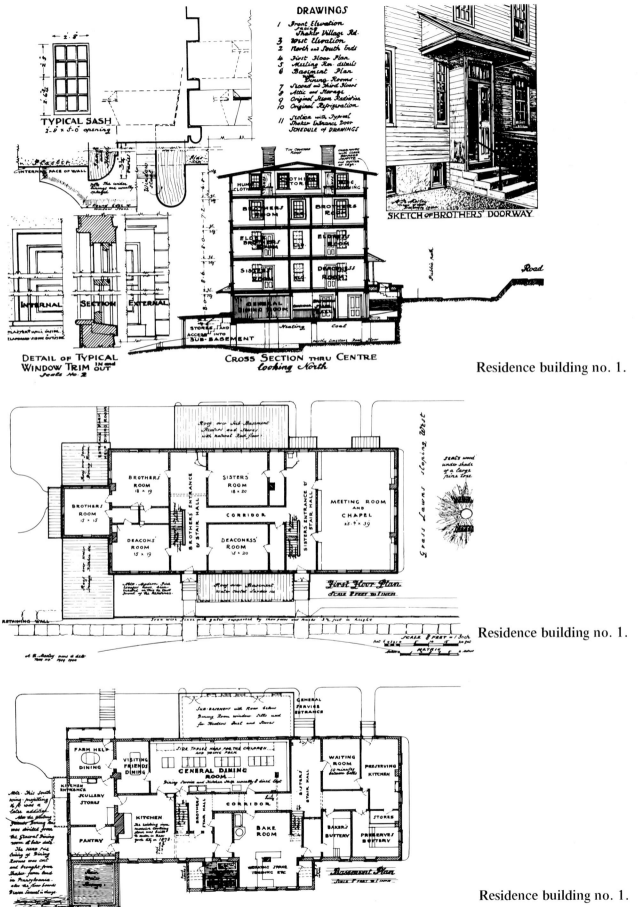

DRAWINGS

1. Front Elevation facing Shaker Village Rd.
3. West Elevation
2. North and South Ends
4. First Floor Plan
5. Meeting Rm. details
6. Basement Plan Dining Rooms
7. Second and Third Floors
8. Attic and Storage
9. Original Steam Radiation
10. Original Refrigeration
11. Section with Typical Shaker Entrance Door
SCHEDULE of DRAWINGS

TYPICAL SASH
2.8 x 5.0 opening

DETAIL of TYPICAL WINDOW TRIM IN and OUT
Scale No. 2

INTERNAL   SECTION   EXTERNAL

CROSS SECTION thru CENTRE looking North

SKETCH of BROTHERS' DOORWAY

Residence building no. 1.

First Floor Plan

Residence building no. 1.

Basement Plan

Residence building no. 1.

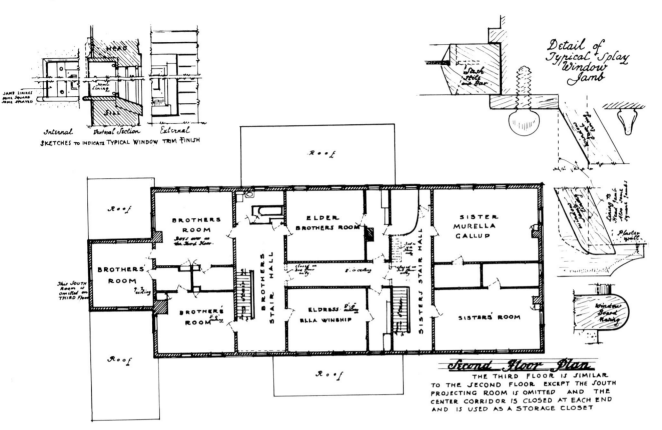

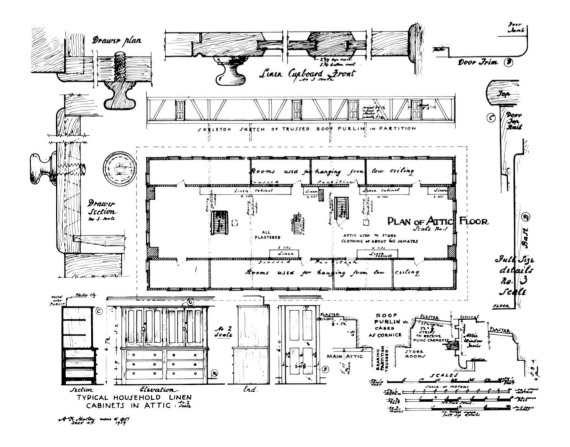

Residence building no. 1.

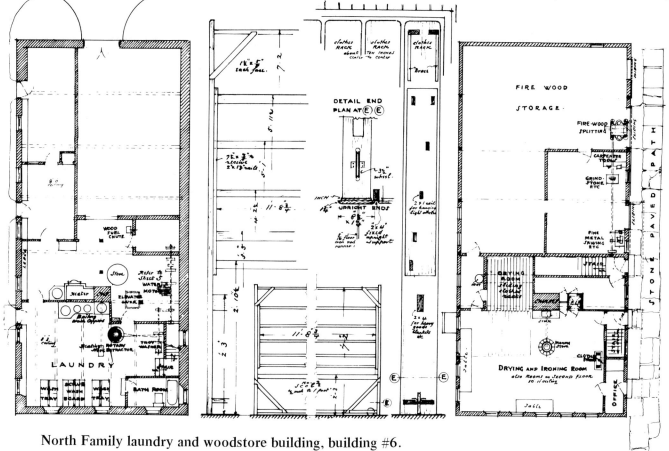

North Family laundry and woodstore building, building #6.

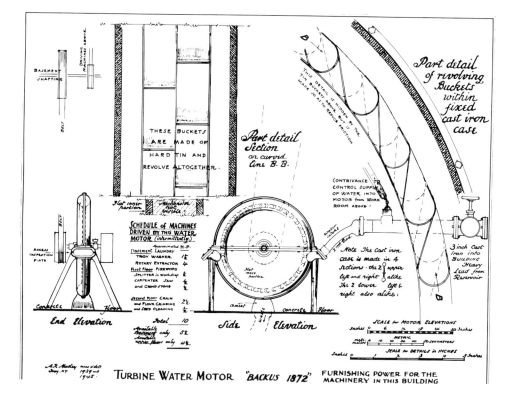

Laundry and woodstore building no. 6.

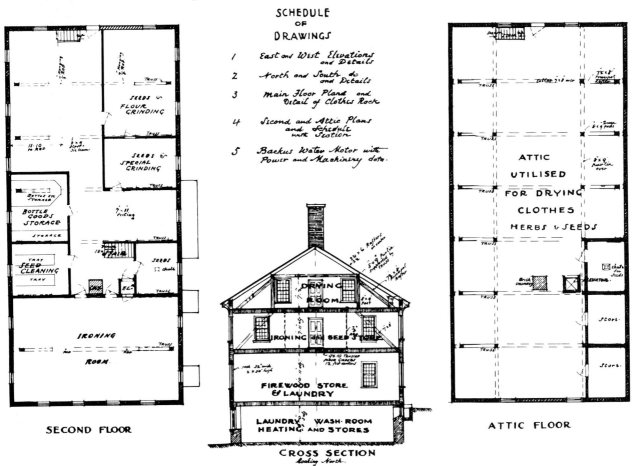

SECOND FLOOR

SCHEDULE OF DRAWINGS

1   East and West Elevations and Details

2   North and South do and Details

3   Main Floor Plans and Detail of Clothes Rack

4   Second and Attic Plans and Schedule with Section

5   Backus Water Motor with Power and Machinery dots.

CROSS SECTION
looking North.

ATTIC UTILISED FOR DRYING CLOTHES HERBS & SEEDS

ATTIC FLOOR

North Family laundry and woodstore building, building #6. Ironing room with drying racks.

William F. Winter, Jr., Photographer

N. E. Baldwin, Photographer

North Family laundry and woodstore building,
building #6. Laundry kettles.

N. E. Baldwin, Photographer

North Family laundry and woodstore building, building #6. Sheet press.

N. E. Baldwin, Photographer

North Family laundry and woodstore building, building #6. Grindstone and circular saw.

N. E. Baldwin, Photographer

North Family "Second Building", building #7. East and north (right) sides.

North Family "Second Building", building #7. Second floor fireplace.

North Family "Second Building", building # 7. Attic with joining chimneys.

North Family barn, building # 14. East side.

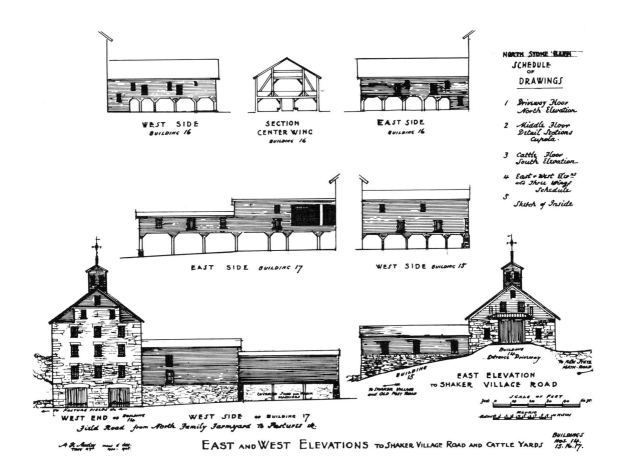

WEST SIDE
BUILDING 16

SECTION
CENTER WING
BUILDING 16

EAST SIDE
BUILDING 16

NORTH STONE BARN
SCHEDULE
OF
DRAWINGS

1 Driveway Floor
   North Elevation

2 Middle Floor
   Detail Sections
   Cupola.

3 Cattle Floor
   South Elevation

4 East & West Elev.ns
   and Three Wings
   Schedule

5 Sketch of Inside

EAST SIDE BUILDING 17

WEST SIDE BUILDING 15

WEST END OF BUILDING 14

WEST SIDE OF BUILDING 17

Field Road from North Family Farmyard to Pastures etc.

COVERED SHED FOR FARM MACHINERY

BUILDING 15
TO SHAKER VILLAGE
AND OLD POST ROAD

BUILDING 14
Entrance Driveway

TO NEW STATE
MAIN ROAD

EAST ELEVATION
TO SHAKER VILLAGE ROAD

SCALE OF FEET

EAST AND WEST ELEVATIONS TO SHAKER VILLAGE ROAD AND CATTLE YARDS

BUILDINGS
NOS. 14,
15, 16, 17.

North Family barn, building # 14. South sides.

William F. Winter, Jr., Photographer

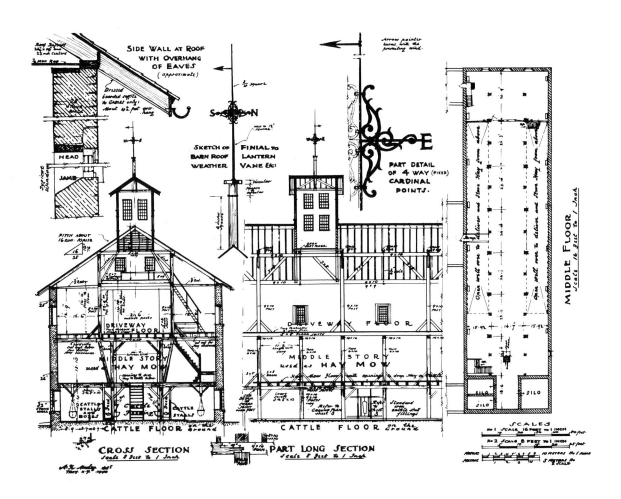

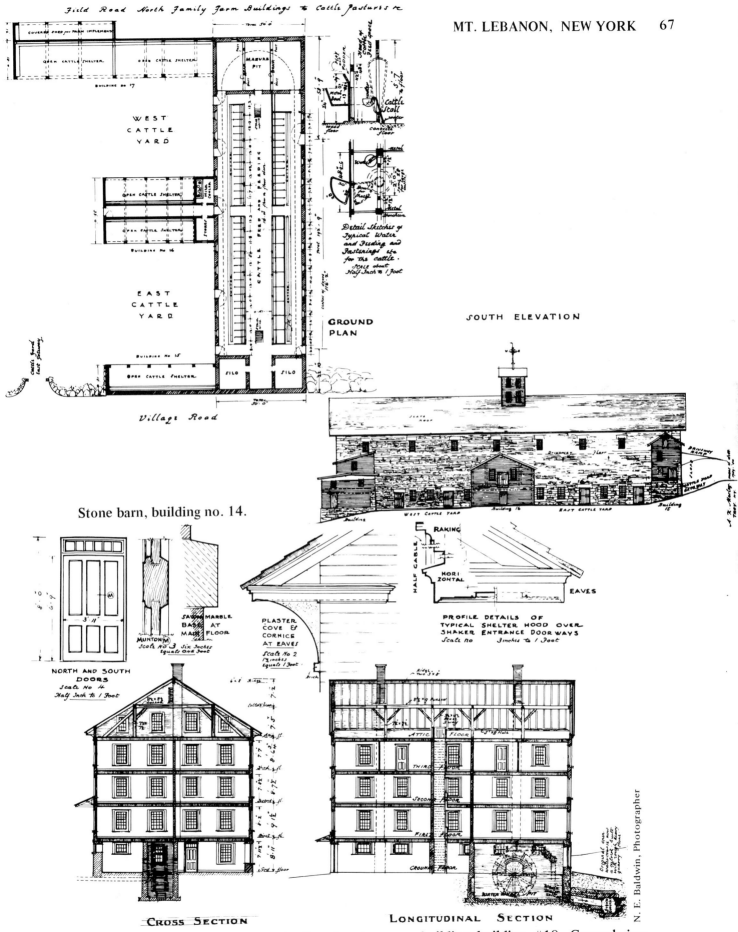

Field Road North Family Farm Buildings to Cattle Pastures &c

COVERED SHED FOR FARM IMPLEMENTS

OPEN CATTLE SHELTER   OPEN CATTLE SHELTER

BUILDING NO 17

WEST
CATTLE
YARD

MANURE PIT

OPEN CATTLE SHELTER

OPEN CATTLE SHELTER

BUILDING NO 16

EAST
CATTLE
YARD

CATTLE FEED AND FEEDING

BUILDING NO 15

OPEN CATTLE SHELTER   SILO   SILO

Village Road

GROUND PLAN

Cattle Stall

Detail Sketches of
Typical Water
and Feeding and
Fastenings &c
for the cattle.
Scale about
Half Inch to 1 foot

SOUTH ELEVATION

WEST CATTLE YARD   Building 16   EAST CATTLE YARD   Building 15

Stone barn, building no. 14.

NORTH AND SOUTH DOORS
Scale No 4
Half Inch to 1 Foot

MUNTON (M)
Scale No 3 Six Inches Equals ONE Foot

SAVON MARBLE BASE AT MAIN FLOOR

PLASTER COVE & CORNICE AT EAVES
Scale No 2
1½ inches Equals 1 Foot

RAKING

HALF GABLE

HORI ZONTAL

EAVES

PROFILE DETAILS OF TYPICAL SHELTER HOOD OVER SHAKER ENTRANCE DOORWAYS
Scale No   3 inches to 1 Foot

ATTIC FLOOR

THIRD FLOOR

SECOND FLOOR

FIRST FLOOR

GROUND FLOOR

CROSS SECTION

LONGITUDINAL SECTION

N. E. Baldwin, Photographer

North Family laundry (original) and water power building, building #18. General view.

William F. Winter, Jr., Photographer

North Family laundry (original) and water power building, building #18. Storage room.

C. C. Adams, Photographer

North Family laundry (original) and water power building, building #18. Seed packing room.

North Family laundry (original) and water power building, building #18. Attic with broom and static machines.

Laundry and water power building no. 18.

North Family Smithy, building #19. General view with Brethren's shop to left.   N. E. Baldwin, Photographer

North Family Smithy, building #19. Smithy forge.

N. E. Baldwin, Photographer

William F. Winter, Jr., Photographer

North Family Smithy, building #19. Smithy forge.

North Family Smithy, building #19. Smithy bellows.

William F. Winter, Jr., Photographer

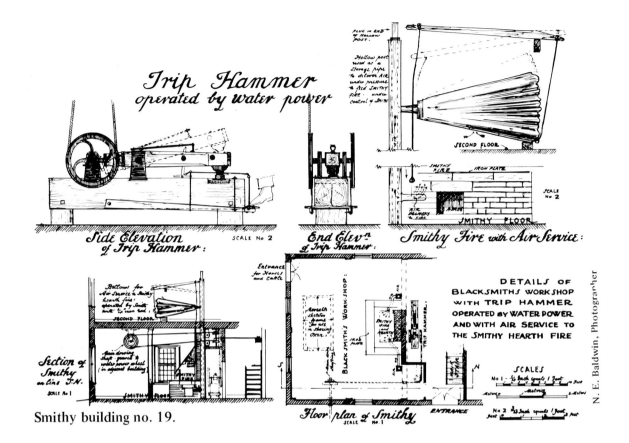

Trip Hammer operated by water power

Side Elevation of Trip Hammer :   SCALE No 2

End Elevⁿ of Trip Hammer :

Smithy Fire with Air Service :

Section of Smithy on line S.N.

Smithy building no. 19.

Floor plan of Smithy

DETAILS OF
BLACKSMITHS WORKSHOP
WITH TRIP HAMMER
OPERATED BY WATER POWER
AND WITH AIR SERVICE TO
THE SMITHY HEARTH FIRE

SCALES

N. E. Baldwin, Photographer

North Family Lumber and Grist Mill, building #20. South and east (front) sides.

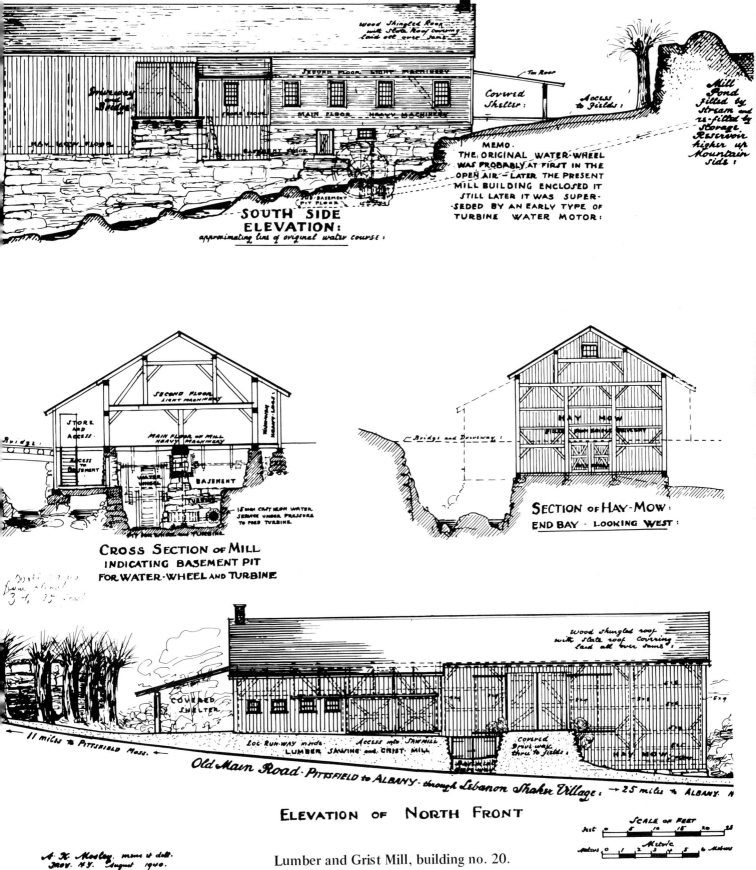

SOUTH SIDE ELEVATION:
approximating line of original water course:

MEMO.
THE ORIGINAL WATER-WHEEL WAS PROBABLY AT FIRST IN THE OPEN AIR - LATER THE PRESENT MILL BUILDING ENCLOSED IT - STILL LATER IT WAS SUPER-SEDED BY AN EARLY TYPE OF TURBINE WATER MOTOR:

CROSS SECTION of MILL
INDICATING BASEMENT PIT
FOR WATER-WHEEL and TURBINE

SECTION of HAY-MOW:
END BAY · LOOKING WEST:

ELEVATION of NORTH FRONT

Lumber and Grist Mill, building no. 20.

North Family Granary. General view.

South Family. General view: office left, barn center.

William F. Winter, Jr., Photographer

South Family dwelling house, building #1. Built-in cupboard.

South Family dwelling house, building #1. Sister's room.

William F. Winter, Jr., Photographer

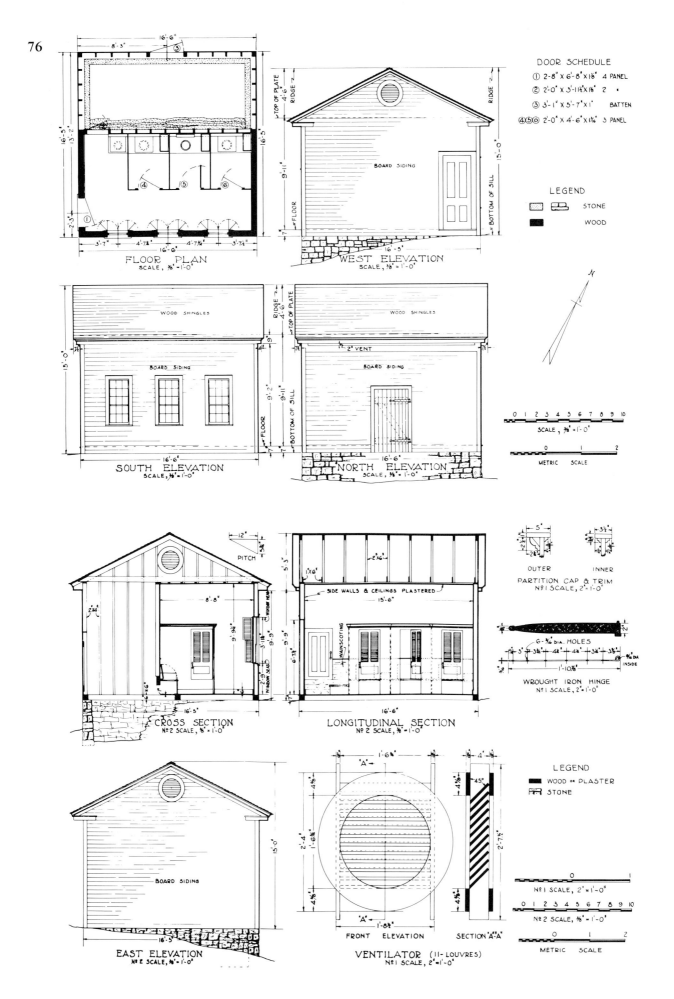

76

DOOR SCHEDULE
① 2'-8" X 6'-8" X 1⅛" 4 PANEL
② 2'-0" X 3'-11¼" X 1⅛" 2 "
③ 3'-1" X 5'-7" X 1" BATTEN
④⑤⑥ 2'-0" X 4'-6" X 1⅜" 3 PANEL

LEGEND
▨ STONE
▨ WOOD

FLOOR PLAN
SCALE, ⅜" = 1'-0"

WEST ELEVATION
SCALE, ⅜" = 1'-0"

BOARD SIDING

SOUTH ELEVATION
SCALE, ⅜" = 1'-0"

WOOD SHINGLES

BOARD SIDING

NORTH ELEVATION
SCALE, ⅜" = 1'-0"

WOOD SHINGLES

2" VENT

BOARD SIDING

N

0 1 2 3 4 5 6 7 8 9 10
SCALE, ⅜" = 1'-0"

0 1 2
METRIC SCALE

CROSS SECTION
N° 2 SCALE, ⅜" = 1'-0"

PITCH

SIDE WALLS & CEILINGS PLASTERED

WAINSCOTING

LONGITUDINAL SECTION
N° 2 SCALE, ⅜" = 1'-0"

OUTER   INNER
PARTITION CAP & TRIM
N° 1 SCALE, 2" = 1'-0"

6 - ⅜" DIA. HOLES
WROUGHT IRON HINGE
N° 1 SCALE, 2" = 1'-0"

EAST ELEVATION
N° 2 SCALE, ⅜" = 1'-0"

BOARD SIDING

FRONT ELEVATION   SECTION 'A'-'A'
VENTILATOR (11- LOUVRES)
N° 1 SCALE, 2" = 1'-0"

LEGEND
▬ WOOD or PLASTER
▥ STONE

0 1
N° 1 SCALE, 2" = 1'-0"

0 1 2 3 4 5 6 7 8 9 10
N° 2 SCALE, ⅜" = 1'-0"

0 1 2
METRIC SCALE

South Family, building #6. West (front) and south sides, with chair shop to right.

South Family, building #6. Main entry.

Jack Boucher, Photographer

William F. Winter, Jr., Photographer

South Family. Laundry and Sisters' chairmaking shop, building #6. Chair showroom.

South Family. Laundry and Sisters' chairmaking shop, building #6. Interior view.

William F. Winter, Jr., Photographer

South Family. Laundry and Sisters' chairmaking shop, building #6. Loom room.

William F. Winter, Jr., Photographer

William F. Winter, Jr., Photographer

South Family. Chair shop, building #7. North elevation.

Center Family. General view from west.

William F. Winter, Jr., Photographer

Center Family Medicine Factory. North and south elevations.

Center Family Medicine Factory. Extracting room.

Center Family Smithy, building # 15. North and east sides.

Second Family dwelling house. East (front) side.

Second Family dwelling house. Stairway on second floor.

William F. Winter, Jr., Photographer

Second Family chair factory. East (front) side.

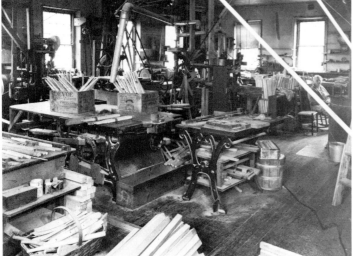

N. E. Baldwin, Photographer

Second Family chair factory. Chair shop from southwest corner.

Second Family chair factory. Northwest corner of chair shop.

N. E. Baldwin, Photographer

Second family herb house, building destroyed by fire c. 1850. Photocopy of an old stereogram.

Caanan Family, view of shops.

Chapter 3
Hancock, Massachusetts

1790–1960

Location: Junction of U.S. Route 20 and State
Route 41, 5 miles west of Pittsfield.

In 1790 the third Shaker community was founded at Hancock, Massachusetts, just a few miles across the state line from Mount Lebanon. Daniel Goodrich, on whose farm the Society was located, was the son of a Baptist deacon and one of twelve brothers, most of whom, with their neighbors, joined the Shaker sect. As one of the earliest communities, Hancock was subject to some of the harshest persecution at the hands of nonbelievers. In August 1783, when Mother Ann and a group of elders came to visit the incipient community at Hancock, they found a hostile mob waiting for them. They were served with a warrant, fined for disturbing the peace, and ordered to leave the state. When they refused to do so, their supporters were imprisoned. Soon thereafter Mother Ann and the elders were again attacked by an angry mob, which temporarily drove them from the state.

Several years after Mother Ann's death, Hancock was "gathered" under the leadership of Calvin Harlow and Sarah Harrison. Several personal accounts of those early years left by Hancock Shakers describe a life of poverty, deprivation, and ceaseless toil. However, gradually they began to prosper and with prosperity came the respect and admiration of their neighbors. In time the village acquired 300 members and 3,000 acres of land, and developed a number of industries including the production of seeds, herbs, and patent medicines, and the manufacturing of brooms, swifts, pails, stoves, and tinware. It was for the latter that the Hancock Shakers were particularly well known, as well as for their famous round barn, according to oral tradition designed by Daniel Goodrich.

In 1960, when few Shakers remained at Hancock, the parent ministry at Canterbury put the property up for sale. The non-profit corporation Shaker Village, Inc., was formed to acquire it. The corporation has restored most of the Church Family and opened it to the public as a museum.

Church Family. General view looking northeast.   Elmer R. Pearson, Photographer

Church Family. General view looking southeast.   Elmer R. Pearson, Photographer

Church Family. General view from east.   Jack E. Boucher, Photographer

Church Family Brethren's shop. South elevation. Built before 1833, the Brethren's shop appears in a watercolor chart of the Church Family area, dated 1833. The building is a typical post and beam framing, all is original to the structure. There is a heavy ridge member and purlins supporting the rafters at mid-span which in turn are supported by means of connecting columns by the second floor ceiling girders. The columns and girders are either encased in finished boards or are neatly chamfered and finished in all finished areas. The building is planned symmetrically, with a central stairway and one room on each side on both the first and second floors. These rooms have been divided into smaller areas at different times. The attic and cellar stairs are original, but the first to second floor stairs have been added and the rise made more gentle.

Mrs. Morris Austin, formerly a Shaker sister at Hancock, reported that the building had several uses: one room was used as a school room, another area as a coffin storage, another as a clock repair shop, one room as a carpentry shop, etc.. In a sketch made early in the century by a Williams College student, by the name of Wright, (now in the Williams College library), the building is called a shoe shop. Table swifts were also made here.

Jack E. Boucher, Photographer

Church Family Dairy and Weave shop. North elevation, showing window and door detail.

Jack E. Boucher, Photographer

Church Family Brethren's Shop. Bathtub enclosure, second
    floor, west room, east wall.

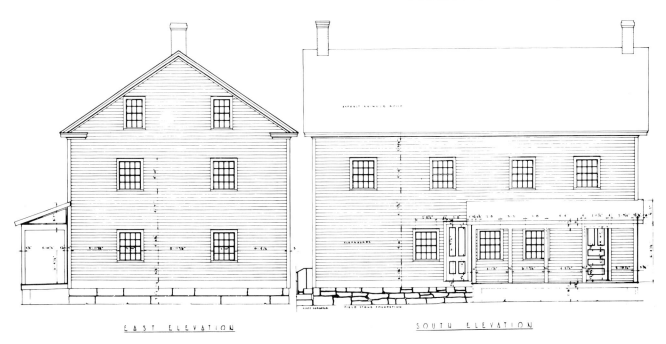

EAST ELEVATION   SOUTH ELEVATION

Dairy and Weave shop.

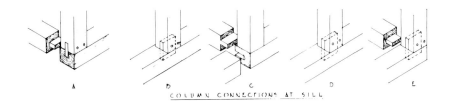

A   B   C   D   E
COLUMN CONNECTIONS AT SILL

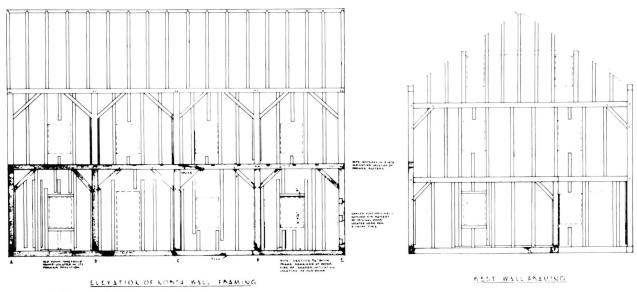

ELEVATION OF NORTH WALL FRAMING   WEST WALL FRAMING

Dairy and Weave shop.

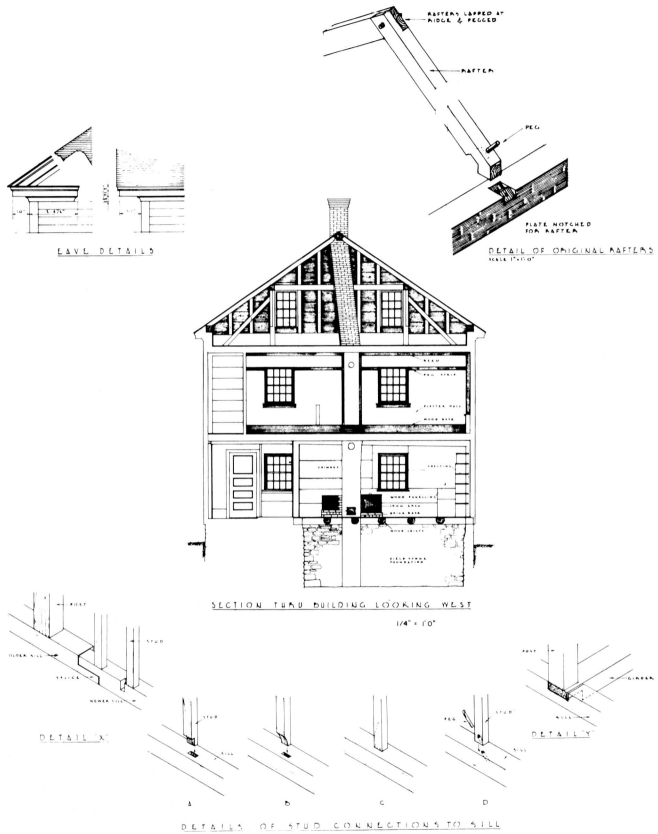

RAFTERS LAPPED AT RIDGE & PEGGED

RAFTER

PEG

PLATE NOTCHED FOR RAFTER

DETAIL OF ORIGINAL RAFTERS
SCALE 1"=1'-0"

EAVE DETAILS

SECTION THRU BUILDING LOOKING WEST
1/4" = 1'0"

DETAIL "X"

POST

STUD

OLDER SILL

SPLICE

NEWER SILL

A   B   C   D

STUD

SILL

PEG

STUD

SILL

DETAIL "Y"

POST

GIRDER

SILL

DETAILS OF STUD CONNECTIONS TO SILL

Dairy and Weave shop.

Jack E. Boucher, Photographer

Church Family main dwelling house. East facade.

Elmer R. Pearson, Photographer

Church Family main dwelling house.
Side elevation, looking north.

Church Family main dwelling house. View from
round barn to dwelling.

Brick arches in basement.

Kitchen, ground level, looking east.

Kitchen, ground level, looking northwest.

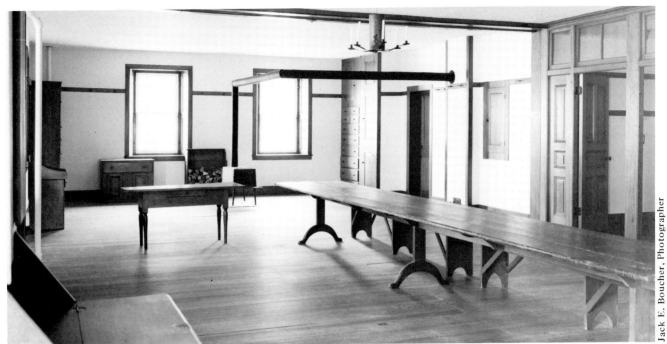

Church Family main dwelling house. Large room (probably meeting room), north end of first floor.

Jack E. Boucher, Photographer

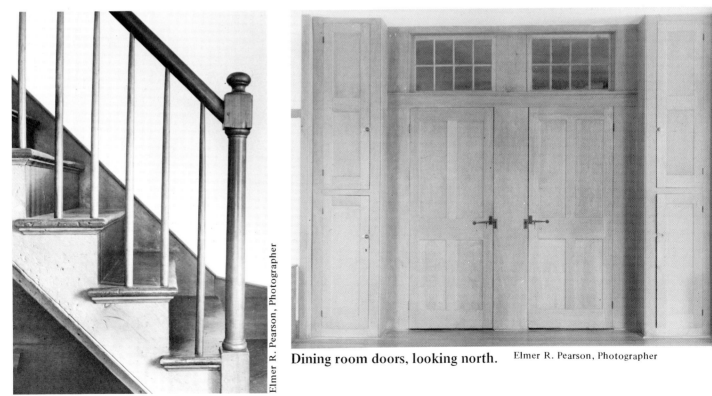

Rear stair hall, ground level.

Dining room doors, looking north.   Elmer R. Pearson, Photographer

Elmer R. Pearson, Photographer

Jack E. Boucher, Photographer

Church Family main dwelling house. Restored schoolroom, second floor.

Jack E. Boucher, Photographer

Stairs to second floor, east side of first floor.

Jack E. Boucher, Photographer

Built-in cabinet with Shaker stove in foreground.

Church Family main dwelling house. Interior of elders' room, showing Shaker furniture and stove.

Sewing room.

Interior showing typical Shaker furniture and heating stove.

Church Family main dwelling house. Stair rail and baluster detail, second to third floor, south end of building.

Stair and well detail, center of building, third floor.

Hall, third floor, looking north.

Elmer R. Pearson, Photographer

Church Family main dwelling house.
Built-in storage units, first attic,
looking northeast.

Elmer R. Pearson, Photographer

Attic stair, top level.

Elmer R. Pearson, Photographer

Second attic, looking north.

Church Family frame barn. Elevation, looking west.

Church Family icehouse. Elevation, looking southwest.

Church Family icehouse. Front and side elevations.

N. E. Baldwin, Photographer

Church Family Sisters' Shop. Elevation.

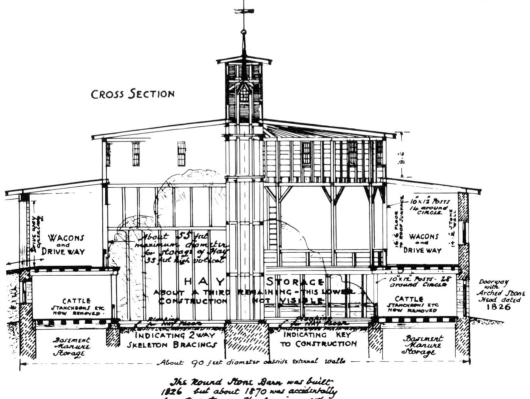

CROSS SECTION

WACONS
and
DRIVE WAY

10"x12" POSTS
14 around
CIRCLE.

WACONS
and
DRIVE WAY

About 55 feet
maximum diameter
for storage of Hay
35 feet high vertical

HAY   STORAGE
ABOUT A THIRD REMAINING - THIS LOWER
CONSTRUCTION   NOT VISIBLE

10"x12" POSTS - 28
around CIRCLE.

Doorway
with
Arched Stone
Head dated
1826

CATTLE
STANCHEONS ETC
NOW REMOVED

INDICATING 2 WAY
SKELETON BRACINGS

INDICATING KEY
TO CONSTRUCTION

CATTLE
STANCHEONS ETC
NOW REMOVED

Basement
Manure
Storage

Basement
Manure
Storage

About 90 feet diameter outside external walls

The Round Stone Barn was built
1826 but about 1870 was accidentally
burnt out The framing of the
structure was replaced by new.

Hancock Shakers round barn.

Jack E. Boucher, Photographer

Church Family round barn. North elevation.

Jack E. Boucher, Photographer

Church Family round barn. View of interior framing.

Elmer R. Pearson, Photographer

Church Family round barn. View looking southwest.

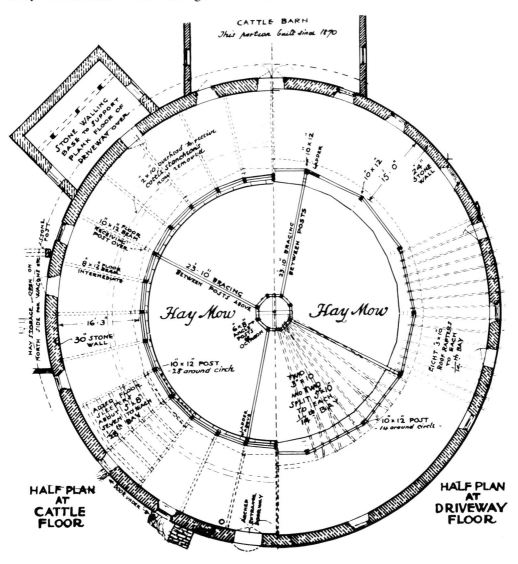

N. E. Baldwin, Photographer

Church Family round barn. North side, entrance to manure level.

N. E. Baldwin, Photographer

Church Family round barn. North side, doors to main floor.

Church Family Tannery. View looking northeast.

Window and shutter detail on two ground floor windows, west side.

Door to ground floor, with detail of lights, west side.

Church Family Trustees' Office. View looking northwest.

Church Family washhouse and machine shop. North elevation.

Elmer R. Pearson, Photographer

Church Family washhouse and machine shop. View looking west.

Jack E. Boucher, Photographer

Room, first floor, west end, showing flatiron heating stove.

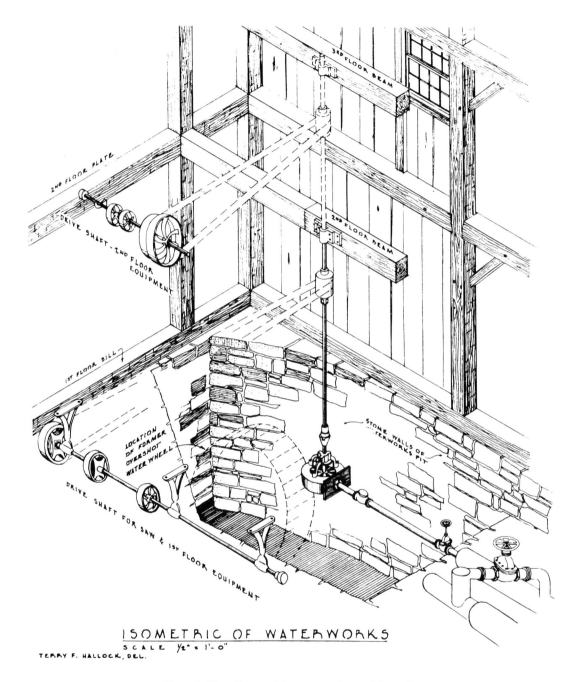

ISOMETRIC OF WATERWORKS
SCALE ½" = 1'-0"
TERRY F. HALLOCK, DEL.

Church Family washhouse and machine shop.

Jack E. Boucher, Photographer

Church Family washhouse and machine shop. Laundry drying room, second floor, west end.

William F. Winter, Jr., Photographer

Church Family washhouse and machine shop. Ironing stove.

William F. Winter, Jr., Photographer

Meetinghouse (first). Side and front.

William F. Winter, Jr., Photographer

Meetinghouse (first). Interior of meeting room.

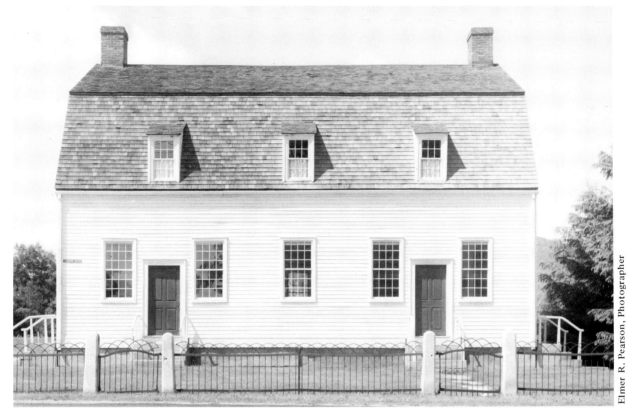

Meetinghouse (second). Elevation, looking north.

Ministry's Shop. Side elevation, looking west.

Ministry's Washhouse, building #4. View from southwest.

Interior view, showing typical Shaker iron stove, table.

Chapter 4

Harvard, Massachusetts

1791–1919

Location: Approximately 2 miles west of Worcester-Middlesex County line, 1 mile south of State Route 2A, on Shaker Road.

From the settlement at Niskeyuna, New York, Mother Ann Lee and a small group of followers embarked on a missionary journey through New England in May 1781, pausing for short periods wherever sympathetic listeners could be found among the usually antagonistic crowds. Mother Ann was drawn to Harvard because of the religious fervor in that area, initiated by the radical New Light preacher Shadrach Ireland. A mystical vision directed her to Ireland's "Square House" where she established headquarters for two years, until she was driven from the town by an angry mob.

In spite of the continued hostility of the townspeople, organizers from Mount Lebanon returned in 1791 to help found the Harvard community on the basis Mother Ann had laid ten years earlier. That same year a meetinghouse was erected by Moses Johnson permanently establishing the Shakers in the Harvard area. Father Eleazar Rand and Mother Hannah Kendal were given charge of the development of the community, which prospered, growing to 200 members and 1,800 acres of fine farmlands by 1823. An assortment of industries produced the necessities for the self-sufficient village as well as popular items for sale to the "world": high quality pressed and packed herbs of fifty different types; wooden objects including brooms, boxes, and furniture; and the typical Shaker stoves which were produced at Harvard's own foundry.

Many industries had to be abandoned because of the decline in membership that plagued all Shaker communities at the end of the nineteenth century and the competition that mass production introduced. The South Family area was forced to close and sell their property in 1899, and the remaining "families" were only able to survive until 1918 when they sold the remainder of the Harvard estate. All of the buildings are now occupied under an unusual land tenure system.

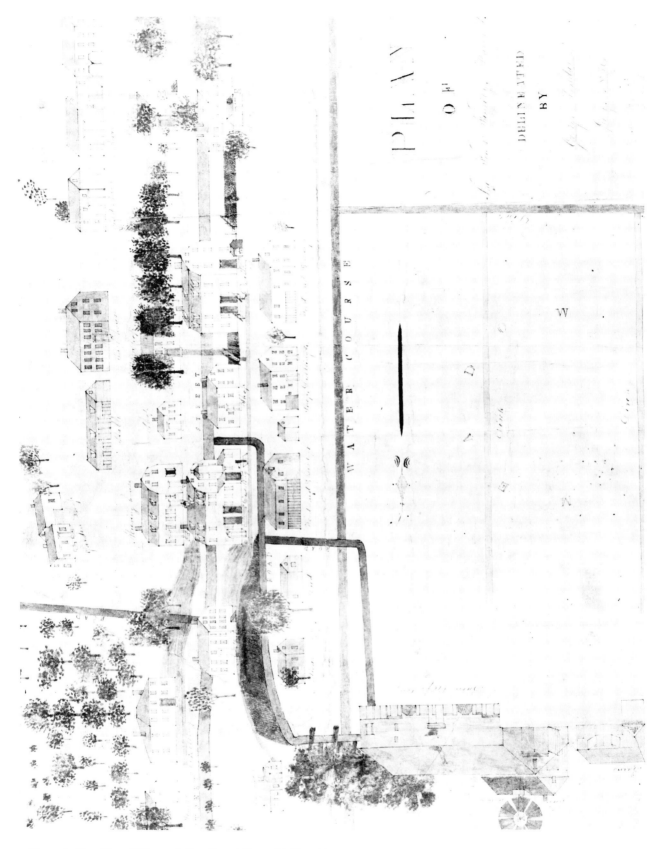

Church Family. "Plan of the first (Church) Family, Harvard", delineated by George Kimball, July, 1836. In Fruitlands Museum, Harvard.

Church Family Meetinghouse. West (front) elevation.

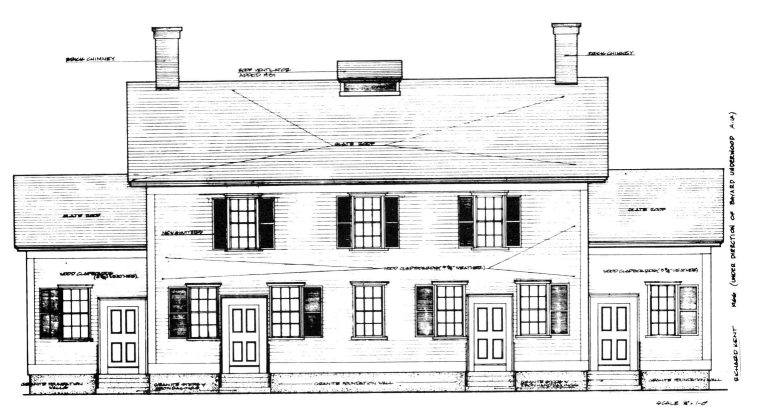

Jack E. Boucher, Photographer

Meetinghouse. Interior doors.

Jack E. Boucher, Photographer

Meetinghouse. Second floor hall, showing entrance to room and recessed cabinet drawers.

Jack E. Boucher, Photographer

Meetinghouse. Interior, north staircase, view from hallway, second floor.

Church Family dwelling house (second).

Church Family dwelling house (second). Bake oven, southeast room, basement.

Church Family Trustee's office (second). West (front) elevation from northwest.

Jack E. Boucher, Photographer

Church Family Trustee's office (second). Cabinets, first floor, southwest room, southeast corner.

Church Family Trustee's office (second). Stairs and hall, second floor, west view.

Church Family Trustee's office (second). Chimney flues from doorway on fourth floor. View is north to south.

Church Family Trustee's office (second). Floor level window, third floor, south side.

Jack E. Boucher, Photographer

Church Family Square House (Shaker Shadrach Ireland House). South (front) elevation from southeast.

Jack E. Boucher, Photographer

Church Family Square House. (Shaker Shadrach Ireland House). Pre-Shaker staircase, showing wood wainscoting and newel post.

Ministry's Shop. South front, oblique view.

Ministry's Shop. Window detail, with recessed vertical sliding wood shutter in open position.

Ministry's Shop. Window detail, showing recessed vertical sliding shutters in closed position.

Jack E. Boucher, Photographer

South Family dwelling house. Northwest view.

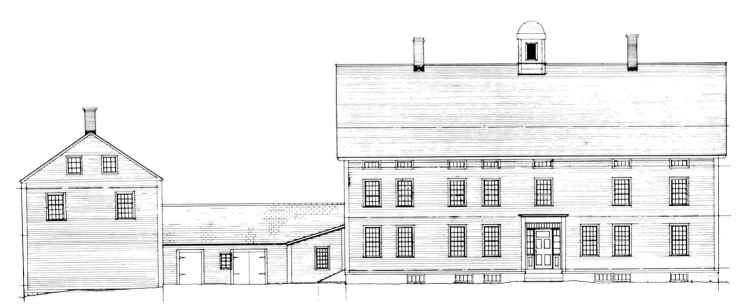

South Family dwelling and washshed.

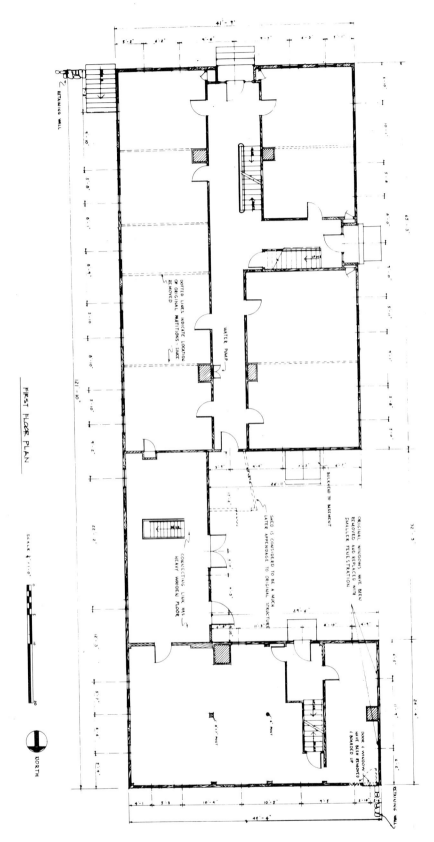

South Family dwelling and washshed.

South Family barn. View from southwest.

South Family barn. Interior, third level, looking west.

Chapter 5
Tyringham, Massachusetts

1792–1875

The Shaker community at Tyringham, Massachusetts was founded in 1792, disbanded in 1875. It was not covered by the H.A.B.S. Surveys. There were three families comprising about one hundred people at its peak.

Fernside. General view.

Mill (in disrepair).

Chapter 6
Enfield, Connecticut

1792–1917

The Shaker community at Enfield, Connecticut was founded in 1792 and disbanded in 1917. It was not covered by the H.A.B.S. Surveys. There were five families comprising about one hundred people at the community's peak. A woodworking bench believed to have been made here about 1840 is now installed at the Fruitlands Museum in Harvard, Massachusetts.

Enfield, Connecticut. General view.

Church Family. General view.

Chapter 7
Canterbury, New Hampshire

1792—Present

Location: Approximately 12 miles northeast of Concord and 4 miles south of the Belknap-Merrimack County line, east of Canterbury, on Shaker Road.

The Canterbury community was founded in 1782 when Mother Ann Lee sent two of her followers to New Hampshire to preach among a group of New Light Baptists living in the Canterbury Hills. Among the converts made at that time were the farmer Benjamin Whitcher and his wife Mary, both of whom became leaders in the Society. The Whitcher farm became the nucleus around which the community grew, eventually encompassing 3,000 acres and attaining a membership of 300 believers, divided into the Church, the Second, the North, and for a brief time, the West Family. Within a few months of the Society's "gathering" in 1792, a meetinghouse, similar to the one at Mount Lebanon, was erected under the direction of Moses Johnson. Thereafter building continued to increase for the next twenty years in order to accommodate the growing community. One historian noted that 1815 was the first year that there was no major construction, repair, or remodeling projects at Canterbury.

Because the poor quality of the soil precluded relying solely on agriculture for their livelihood, the Canterbury Shakers manufactured a variety of farm implements, textiles, and household goods to sell to the "world people", including stoves and washing machines. (It is said that a washing machine was invented at Canterbury and that the patent for it was held by that Society for some time). The community also raised livestock which was generally admired for its fine quality, and for many years served as the publishing center for the northern communities.

In 1875, the American journalist, Charles Nordhoff, recorded upon his visit to Canterbury only 145 members. "They have not gained in numbers in ten years, and few applicants nowadays remain with them." The decline continued gradually over the next century, and today there are only four sisters left at Canterbury. The one remaining North Family building is privately owned, but the Church Family buildings are still occupied by Shakers. In 1973 the non-profit foundation, Shaker Village Inc., was formed to perpetuate the Shaker legacy at Canterbury.

Church Family Creamery (Shaker Church Family Boys' House). View looking southeast. Elmer R. Pearson, Photographer

Church Family. General view.

Miller/Swift, Photographers

Church Family barn and granary. Elevation.

Elmer R. Pearson, Photographer

Church Family dwelling house. View looking north.

Church Family dwelling house. View looking southwest.

Elmer R. Pearson, Photographer

Church Family Trustee's office (Shaker Church Family Enfield office). View looking northeast.

Elmer R. Pearson, Photographer

Church Family Trustee's office (Church Family Enfield house). Detail of porches, looking northeast.

Miller/Swift, Photographers

Church Family Trustee's office (Shaker Church Family Enfield House).

Church Family Schoolhouse. Rear elevation, looking north.   Elmer R. Pearson, Photographer

Church Family Schoolhouse, interior.

Church Family Sugar House.

"It is impossible to describe the air of tran-
quility and comfort that diffuses itself over a
Shaker Settlement.....the two sexes together bear
the burden. if burden it may be. of celibacy.....
The union of these people. their uniform kind-
ness to each other. and the singularly benevolent
and tender expression of their countenances.
speak a stronger language than their professions."

from "The Shakers". *Boston Palladium.* 19 September.
1829. reprinted from the *Niles Weekly Register.*

Church Family Children's House (East House). Elevation.
looking southeast.

Chapter 8

Enfield, New Hampshire

1793–1923

Location: Overlooking Mascoma Lake, 4 miles northwest of Enfield Center, on State Route 4A.

When the two New Lebanon missionaries, Israel Chauncey and Ebenezer Cooley, arrived at Enfield, New Hampshire, in 1782, they were openly received by James Jewett and several of his neighbors, all of whom adopted the Shaker faith after hearing their testimony. In 1787 more converts came to Enfield, eager to consolidate Shaker holdings by purchasing or bartering for land in the area. The story is told of one recalcitrant farmer who refused to sell his land, but was driven away by the noise of the dancing and singing that the Shakers engaged in to change his mind. The Society ultimately acquired about 3,000 acres and 350 members, divided into three "families": the Church Family, the South Family, and the North Family, established in 1793, 1800, and 1812, respectively.

The industries of the Enfield Shakers were not unlike those of other Shaker villages––the production of an assortment of useful household products and farm implements. However, at Enfield, there was more emphasis on the production of textiles. Until the 1840's their mills produced large quantities of linen, cotton, and woolen goods. In addition, they sold applesauce, maple sugar, and patent medicines, and initiated the practice of packaging seeds, which was soon adopted by all the other Shaker communities.

The village was also distinguished in being the home of the architect Moses Johnson, who designed and built meetinghouses in Shaker communities throughout New England, and in having some distinctive architecture of its own. While most Shaker communities erected buildings of frame, brick, or limestone, some of those raised at Enfield were of granite, the most outstanding example being the Church Family Dwelling House, built in 1837. The Shakers have left Enfield, but many of their structures endure. The last seven believers sold the property to the LaSallette Fathers, a Roman Catholic order, and moved to Canterbury in 1923.

Church Family. General view. Copy of photograph taken c. 1904 showing part of the Enfield, New Hampshire Shaker community with the Great Stone House in the center.

Copy photograph: Albern Color Research, Inc.

Church Family machine shop. Elevation, looking southwest.

Elmer R. Pearson, Photographer

Elmer R. Pearson, Photographer

Church Family dwelling house (Great Stone House). Elevation, looking northwest.

Great Stone House. Interior showing original stairway, doors, doorways, and peg strips for hanging furniture.

Aubrey P. Janisn, Photographer

"Whatever is fashioned, let it be plain and simple, unembellished by superfluities which add nothing to its goodness and durability. Think not ye can keep the laws of Zion while blending with the forms and fashions of the children of the unclean."

—Joseph Meacham, c. 1790.

Watercolor paintings by Shaker women using designs of trees, leaves, and branches, 1853.

Chapter 9
Shirley, Massachusetts

1793–1909

Location: North side of U.S. Rt. 20 near intersection with State Rt. 41, 5 miles west of Pittsfield, Hancock, Berkshire County, Massachusetts.

There were three families comprising about
150 members at the peak of the Shirley community which disbanded in 1909. The meetinghouse has been reconstructed at the Hancock,
Massachusetts community where it can be seen
today.

Meetinghouse. Front and side elevations, looking northeast.

Jack E. Boucher, Photographer

Meetinghouse. Door and window detail, south
elevation, during reconstruction.

Elmer R. Pearson, Photographer

Meetinghouse. Detail of doors.

Meetinghouse. Interior, looking north.

Elmer R. Pearson, Photographer

Chapter 10
Alfred, Maine

1793–1932

The first Shaker Society in Maine was at Alfred, founded in 1793. It consisted of three families. In 1808 some North Family members moved to Gorham, Maine, where there was only one family.

In 1819 the community moved to Poland Hill, near Sabbathday Lake, but had to close in 1887. Alfred closed in 1932 and the remaining members moved to Sabbathday Lake.

The buildings at Alfred were erected mostly in three parallel rows, as they felt it suitable for a monastic community. Opposite the meeting house are the Brethren and Sisters' dwelling.

Alfred, Maine. General view.

Alfred, Maine. General view.

Chapter 11

Sabbathday Lake, Maine

New Gloucester, Maine
(Poland Spring)
1794—Present
Location: Approximately 20 miles north of
Portland, west of State Route 26, south of North
Raymond Road.

The New Gloucester Society, later called Sabbathday Lake, was founded during the early 1790's. Nathan Merrill of New Gloucester is reported to have been the first convert. In 1794 he and his neighbors, most of whom were New Light Baptists, and other believers who had joined them were "gathered into society order." Their meetinghouse was erected that same year, the tenth one to be built under the direction of the Shaker architect Moses Johnson. The Society began with a few wooded acres on the side of a hill that sloped down to Sabbathday Lake, and over the years acquired through gifts and its own industry 2,000 acres. Even at its peak Sabbathday Lake had only 150 members, divided into two "families", making it one of the smallest Shaker communities.

The village soon became self-sustaining, the believers having built within the first few years of the Society's founding, a grist mill, a saw mill, linen weaving and carding mills, a tannery, and a coopers' shop. The surplus to be marketed to the "world" was not so much the produce of their fields——as it was in the Shaker settlements farther south——but the products of their mills and machine shops, such as textiles, casks, pails, and spinning wheels. Nordhoff, a nineteenth century journalist, noted in 1875, for example, that their most profitable industry was the manufacture of oak staves for molasses hogsheads which were exported to the West Indies.

Sabbathday Lake's population declined less precipitously than that of the other Shaker societies, even those in Maine. The other two Maine societies were both absorbed by Sabbathday Lake——Gorham in 1819, and Alfred in 1932. Until the 1930's its mills continued to turn out packing cases for the nearby town of Poland, and the last Shaker craftsman, Elder Delmer Wilson, was still producing oval boxes and carriers until the time of his death in 1961.

Sabbathday Lake Community Meetinghouse. View owned by the United Society of Shakers, Sabbathday Lake, Maine — housed in community's Shaker Museum.

Meetinghouse, from *History of Cumberland County, Maine* (Philadelphia: Everts and Peck, 1880), facing page 328.

Gerda Peterich, Photographer

Meetinghouse. East elevation.

Miller/Swift, Photographers

Meetinghouse. Rear elevation and side elevation with stair tower.

Meetinghouse. Gate to north door of Meetinghouse looking east.

Meetinghouse. First floor looking southeast.

Meetinghouse. Interior, looking north.

Church Family barns. Elevations.

Church Family Boys' Shop. Front elevation.

Church Family Washhouse. Front elevation.

Miller/Swift, Photographers

"Rules for Doing Good"

Do all the good you can
In all the ways you can
To all the people you can
In every place you can
At all the times you can
As long as ever you can.

—Found in the Sisters' waiting
room at Sabbathday Lake.

Chapter 12

Union Village, Ohio

(Turtle Creek)
1806–1910

Location: Intersection of State Route 63 and State Route 741, 4 miles west of Lebanon, Warren County.

During the period of religious revival in the midwest area at the beginning of the nineteenth century, Shaker missionaries traveled into this area to gain converts. The first western Shaker community was established in 1806 at Union Village, Ohio.

Isaacher Bates, a missionary from New Lebanon, New York, raised the money to buy land and build the first house at Turtle Creek. The Shakers renamed their community Union Village. Ultimately there were six families here with about six hundred members. The community disbanded in 1910.

Family dwelling. Union Village, Ohio.

South Family dwelling house. Interior.

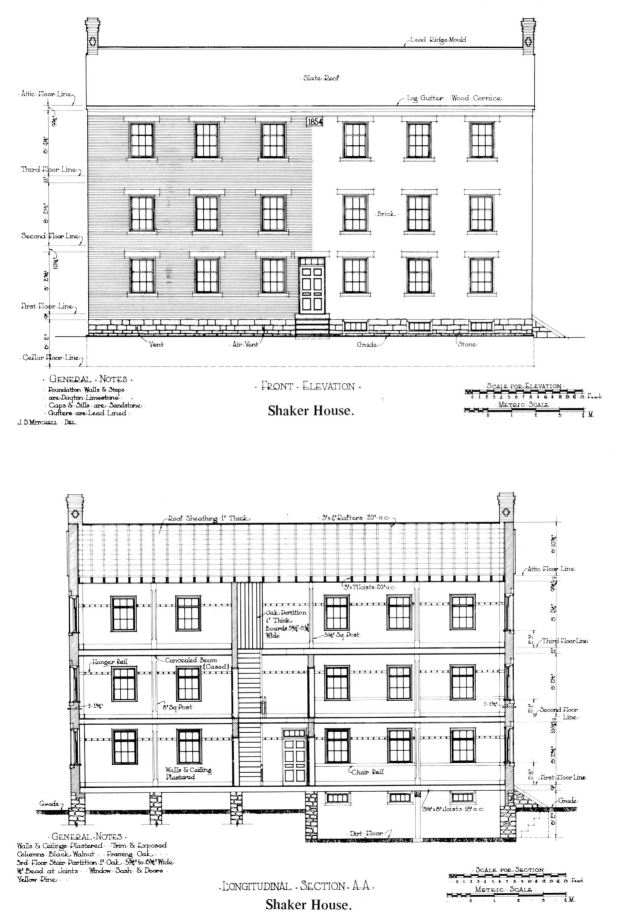

· Lead · Ridge · Mould ·

· Slate · Roof ·

· Log · Gutter · Wood · Cornice ·

· Attic · Floor · Line ·

· Third · Floor · Line ·

1854

· Brick ·

· Second · Floor · Line ·

· First · Floor · Line ·

· Cellar · Floor · Line ·

Vent   Air · Vent   Grade   Stone

· GENERAL · NOTES ·
· Foundation · Walls & · Steps ·
are · Dayton · Limestone ·
· Caps & · Sills · are · Sandstone ·
· Gutters · are · Lead · Lined ·
J. D. Mitchell · Del.

· FRONT · ELEVATION ·

Shaker House.

· SCALE · FOR · ELEVATION ·
0 1 2 3 4 5 6 7 8 9 10 11 12 13 14 15 Feet
METRIC · SCALE ·
0 1 2 3 4 M.

· Roof · Sheathing · 1' · Thick ·   3" x 4" Rafters · 20" o.c.

Attic · Floor · Line

3" x 7" Joists · 20" o.c.

Oak · Partition
1" · Thick
Boards 5¾"-6¾"
Wide

5¼" Sq. Post

Third · Floor Line

Hanger · Rail   Concealed · Beam
(Cased)

Second · Floor
Line

1'-1¾"   8' Sq. Post   1'-1¾"

Walls & Ceiling
Plastered   Chair · Rail

First · Floor Line

Grade   Grade

3¾" x 8" Joists · 18" o.c.

Dirt · Floor

· GENERAL · NOTES ·
Walls & Ceilings · Plastered · · Trim & · Exposed ·
Columns · Black · Walnut · · Framing · Oak ·
3rd · Floor · Stair · Partition · 1' · Oak · 5¾" to 6¾" Wide ·
¼" Bead · at · Joints · · Window · Sash · & · Doors ·
Yellow · Pine ·

· LONGITUDINAL · SECTION · A-A ·

Shaker House.

· SCALE · FOR · SECTION ·
0 1 2 3 4 5 6 7 8 9 10 11 12 13 14 15 Feet
METRIC · SCALE ·
0 1 2 3 4 M.

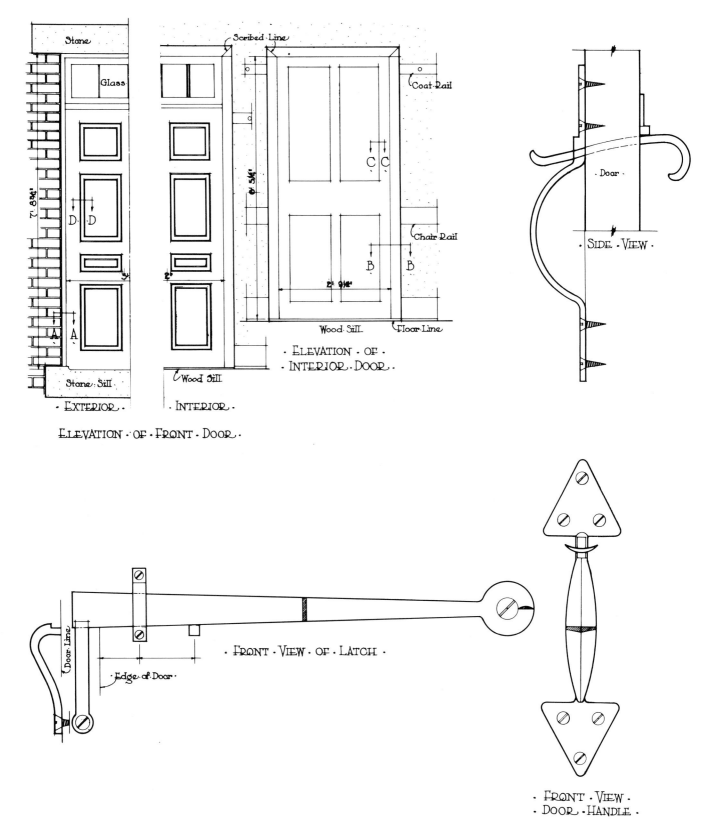

Shaker House.

Chapter 13

South Union, Kentucky

1811–1922

Location: Approximately 15 miles southwest of
Bowling Green, southwest of Warren-Logan
County line, on U.S. Route 68.

South Union at Gasper Springs was founded
during the great Kentucky Revival. The first
converts were New Light Presbyterians, and the
first land was donated in 1807 by Jesse McComb,
a large landholder in Logan County. The community was "gathered into society order" two
or three years later, with the Shaker missionary,
Benjamin Youngs, appointed as its leading elder.
Among the early members were slave-holders,
some of whom prompted their slaves to join the
sect. Consequently, for many years there was a
black "family" at South Union, which was ultimately absorbed into the other three "families"
when it became too small.

The Shakers at South Union eventually owned
about 6,000 acres of land, much of which was
cultivated or planted with orchards, but the community concentrated less on farming and more
on raising livestock. Its cattle, sheep, and chick-
ens were highly regarded in Kentucky and the
surrounding states. The community also manufactured brooms, put up seeds, milled flour, made
preserves from the produce of its own orchards,
and spun silk produced on its own mulberry trees.

The Civil War took a great toll in South Union.
Though they were Union sympathizers, the Shakers cared for soldiers from both sides impartially.
With both Union and Confederate forces moving
back and forth across their land, the Shakers
estimated that they lost over $100,000 in live-
stock, provisions, and buildings. Moreover, they
were compelled to accept thousands of dollars
of worthless Confederate money in payment of
debts. Losses sustained during the War, as well
as subsequent financial losses through unpaid
debts, and a diminishing membership all contrib-
uted to the decline of South Union. In 1922,
when only ten members remained, the estate was
sold at auction for $229,000. The Roman Cath-
olic Order of Saint Benedict purchased the property for use as a monastery in 1949. In 1972,
Shakertown Revisited, Inc., a non-profit educa-
tional corporation, acquired the buildings from
the Benedictines. The corporation is restoring
the community and opening it to the public,
including a yearly festival in July.

Centre Family dwelling house. Elevation from northeast.

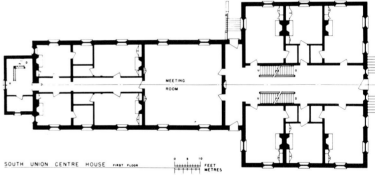

SOUTH UNION CENTRE HOUSE FIRST FLOOR

Centre Family dwelling house. First floor plan.

Centre Family dwelling house. Foot scraper, east side, looking south.

Centre Family dwelling house. Roof detail and stone gutter, east side looking north.

Elmer R. Pearson, Photographer

Elmer R. Pearson, Photographer

Centre Family dwelling house. Doorway, looking northwest.

Elmer R. Pearson, Photographer

Centre Family dwelling house. Iron railing, east side, looking southwest.

Centre Family dwelling house. Rear door, looking south.

Centre Family dwelling house. Front hall, first floor, looking north.

Centre Family dwelling house. First attic, looking northwest.

Elmer R. Pearson, Photographer

Centre Family dwelling house. Stair rail, first attic, looking southeast.

Elmer R. Pearson, Photographer

Elmer R. Pearson, Photographer

Centre Family drying house. Elevation, looking northeast.

Elmer R. Pearson, Photographer

Centre Family washhouse. Elevation from the south.

Ministry's Shop and dwelling. Front elevation, looking south.

Elmer R. Pearson, Photographer

Centre Family washhouse. Elevation, looking east.

Elmer. R. Pearson, Photographer

Elmer R. Pearson, Photographer

Ministry's Shop and dwelling. Entrance stairs, looking southwest.

South Union Tavern (Shaker South Union Hotel). Front elevation looking north.

Elmer R. Pearson, Photographer

Chapter 14

Pleasant Hill, Kentucky

(Shakertown)
(1814–1910)

Location: Northeast of Harrodsburg, north of
U.S. Route 68 and State Route 33 intersection,
on Village Road.

A great religious revival similar in fervor to the one that occurred in New England at the end of the eighteenth century flourished in Kentucky and the surrounding states early in the 1800's. Recognizing the similarity and welcoming the opportunity for new conversions, the Shaker ministry sent missionaries into the area in 1805. After establishing the first western community at Union Village, Ohio, the missionaries traveled south to Kentucky where they founded two more communities at Shawnee Run (Pleasant Hill) and Gasper Springs (South Union).

One hundred forty acres of fertile bluegrass land on the Shawnee River, donated by Elisha Thomas, formed the nucleus of the Pleasant Hill community. By 1820 the community had amassed 4,200 acres and numbered almost 500 members. During the major years of growth, Micajah Burnett, a young Shaker carpenter, served as principal architect and general planner. His fine work was noted by several nineteenth century chroniclers and today Pleasant Hill still provides an outstanding example of Shaker community planning and architecture.

Farming, preserving fruits, and raising livestock provided the economic base for the community. Pleasant Hill also manufactured brooms and other goods and produced silk to be marketed in the "world", but as their population decreased they no longer had the manpower or the economic need to continue. The Civil War, in particular, precipitated the decline of the community. As egalitarians, the Shakers were opposed to slavery and sympathetic to the Union cause, but during the War they were preyed upon by both armies for food and provisions. The War exhausted their supplies and claimed some of their men. By 1875 there were only 245 Shakers left at Pleasant Hill; thirty-five years later, in 1910, the Society was dissolved, when Colonel Bohon of nearby Harrodsburg purchased what remained of the Shaker property. Over the next fifty years the dwellings and shops were leased to various tenants until, in 1961, Shakertown at Pleasant Hill, Inc. was formed to purchase the community for restoration. Many of the buildings are now restored, and the village is open to the public as a museum.

Lester Jones, Photographer

Church Family house. View from northeast.

Lester Jones, Photographer

Church Family house. South entrance detail.

Lester Jones, Photographer

Church Family house. Dining room door (first floor).

Church Family house. Double stairway from second floor.

Lester Jones, Photographer

Meetinghouse. North (front) elevation.

Jack E. Boucher, Photographer

Water Tower building.

Water Tower building. View from southeast.

Lester Jones, Photographer

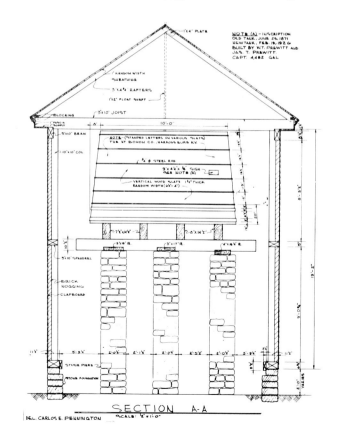

Silk Worm house. View from southwest.

Coopers' Shop (North Family workshop).
South (front) elevation from southeast.

Ministry's Shop. North (front) elevation.

Pleasant Hill before restoration, about 1961.

Centre Family dwelling house. South (front) elevation.

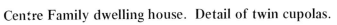

Centre Family dwelling house.

Centre Family dwelling house. Detail of twin cupolas.

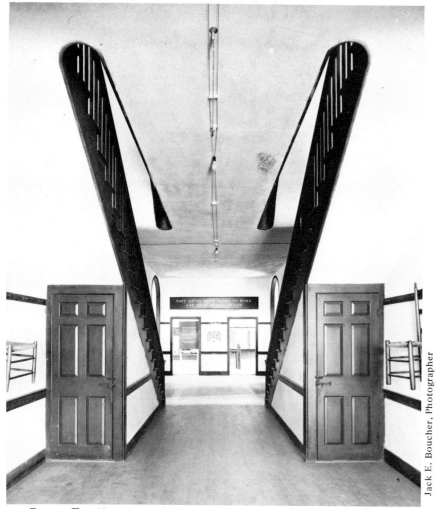

Centre Family dwelling house.   Staircases, first floor, looking north.

Centre Family dwelling house.   Staircases, second floor, looking north.

Centre Family dwelling house, 1824-1834. Kitchen door.

Centre Family dwelling house. View east through doors.

Meetinghouse. Meetingroom, right.

Centre Family Trustees' office. East (side) elevation and south (rear) elevation.

Centre Family Trustees' office. Front entrance and stair hall.

Centre Family Trustees' office. Spiral stairs.

Centre Family Trustees' office. Spiral stairs and egg-shell dormer.

Centre Family Trustees' office. Spiral stairs.

Centre Family Trustees' office. Recessed cabinets and drawers, first floor.

Jack E. Boucher, Photographer

East Family dwelling house. South (front) elevation from south.

Jack E. Boucher, Photographer

East Family dwelling house. East (side) elevation and north (rear) elevation from northeast.

East Family dwelling house. Entrance door, window and brick bond detail, iron stair rail, east rear.

East Family Brethren's shop. South
(front) elevation from south.

Jack E. Boucher, Photographer

West Family house. View from southwest.

Lester Jones, Photographer

West Family house. View from northeast.

Lester Jones, Photographer

West Family Sisters' shop. South (front) elevation and west (side) elevation.

West Family privy. South front and east side.

West Family drying house. North (front) elevation and west (side) elevation.

Chapter 15

Whitewater, Ohio

1824–1907

Location: Northwest of Cincinnati, south of the
Butler-Hamilton County line, on Oxford Road.

The Shakers at Union Village, Ohio, sent
missionaries to the dry fork of the Whitewater
River near the Kentucky-Indiana border at the
behest of Miriam Agnew, a new member of their
community, who told them of the general dis-
satisfaction that prevailed at Whitewater in the
aftermath of a Methodist revival. Within the year,
thirty converts had been made at Whitewater and
the basis for a new community established on
forty acres of uncleared land. In 1824 the decision was made to transfer the faltering Shaker
community at Darby Plains in central Ohio to
Whitewater. The Darby settlers were, by origin,
New Light believers from Vermont and Connecticut who had migrated to Ohio sometime after
1801 and had recently taken up the Shaker belief
after the example of their leader, Nathan Burl-
ingame. Their efforts to build a community at
Darby Plains had been thwarted by disease and
land disputes, so they welcomed the opportunity
to join with their brethren at Whitewater. The
years immediately after the two communities
were "gathered" at Whitewater in 1824 were diffi-
cult, but with the help of the Shakers at Union
Village, new land was acquired, permanent dwellings constructed, and an abundant crop harvested
by 1826. The next year some of the inhabitants
of the recently dissolved Busro, Indiana community joined the Shakers at Whitewater, and a
meetinghouse was raised.

The Whitewater Society ultimately acquired
1,500 acres, but it remained relatively small in
numbers, having at its height only 150 members
divided into three "families". Throughout most
of the nineteenth century it remained fairly
prosperous through farming, breeding livestock,
manufacturing brooms, and putting up garden
seeds. Among the other Shaker communities,
Whitewater was particularly regarded for the
expertise of its bookbinders.

The general dissolution of Shakerdom seems
to have affected the Ohio settlements first, for
at the turn of the century there were only
ninety Shakers left in the state. The decision to
dissolve Whitewater was made in 1907.

North Family. General view across farm field from southeast.

Meetinghouse. View from northeast.

Jack E. Boucher, Photographer

North Family dwelling house. View from southeast.

North Family milk house. View from southeast.

North Family seed house. View from southeast.

North Family woodshed. View from northeast.

Jack E. Boucher, Photographer

Jack E. Boucher, Photographer

Chapter 16
Groveland, New York

(Sonyea)
(Sodus Point)
1826–1892

In 1826 the Groveland, New York Family gathered at Sodus Point and later moved to Sonyea.

Groveland was dissolved in 1892. Objects from Groveland were purchased by New York State shortly after Watervliet Colony was acquired in the early 1930's.

THE SEWING HOUSE.

FRUIT HOUSE AND LAUNDRY.

1 OFFICE
2 HORSE BARN
3 MEETING HOUSE
4 DWELLING HOUSE
5 SEWING HOUSE
6 DINING ROOM & DAIRY

7 FRUIT HOUSE & LAUNDRY
8 STOCK BARN
9 WOOD & CARRIAGE HOUSE
10 BOILER HOUSE
11 JOINER SHOP
12 BROOM SHOP
13 SCHOOL HOUSE

THE HOME OF THE SOCIETY OF CHRISTIAN BELIEVERS
VULGARLY CALLED SHAKERS.   SONYEA, LIVINGSTON, Co, N.Y.

Courtesy, Henry Francis duPont Winterthur Museum, The Edward Deming Andrews Memorial Shaker Collection, No. SA237.

Group of Shakers in their buggys at Canterbury, New Hampshire.

"Fancy articles of any kind - superfluously finished, trimmed or ornamented are not suitable for Believers", according to the Millennial Laws.

Bibliography

Adams, Charles C. "New York State Museum's Historical Survey and Collection of the New York Shakers", *New York State Museum Bulletin,* No. 323 (March, 1941), pp. 77-141.

Andrews, Edward Deming. *Shaker Furniture,* New York: Dover Press, 1964.

Andrews, Edward Deming. *The Gift to Be Simple.* New York: Dover Press, 1962.

Andrews, Edward Deming. *The People Called Shakers.* New York: Oxford University Press, 1953.

Andrews, Edward Deming. "The Shaker Manner of Building", *Art in America,* Vol. 48, No. 3 (Fall, 1960), pp. 38-45.

Andrews, Edward Deming and Faith. *Visions of the Healing Sphere.* Charlottesville: University Press of Virginia, 1969.

Clark, Thomas D. *Pleasant Hill in the Civil War.* Pleasant Hill: Pleasant Hill Press, 1972.

Filley, Dorothy M. *Recapturing Wisdom's Valley.* New York: Publishing Center for Cultural Resources, 1976.

Hopping, D.M.C., and Watland, Gerald R. "The Architecture of the Shakers", *Antiques,* Vol. 72, #4- (October 1957), pp. 335-339.

Johnson, Clifton. "The Passing of the Shakers", *Old-Time New England,* XXV, No. 1 (July, 1934), pp. 3-19; and XXV, No. 2 (October 1934); pp. 50-66.

Lassiter, William Lawrence. "A Catalog of Shaker Photographs and Measured Drawings in the Historic Collection of the New York State Education Department, Albany, New York." An unpublished catalog of Shaker material belonging to the University of the State of New York, Division of Archives and History, Albany, New York, 1960. (mimeographed).

Lassiter, William Lawrence. *Shaker Architecture.* New York: Bonanza Books.

Meacham, Joseph, and Wright, Lucy. *Millennial Laws.* New Lebanon: August, 1821 (revised October 1845).

Melcher, Marguerite Fellows. *The Shaker Adventure.* Cleveland: Western Reserve University Press, 1941.

Nordhoff, Charles. *The Communistic Societies of the United States.* New York: Harper and Brothers, 1875.

"The Shakers", *Harper's New Monthly Magazine,* XV, No. 86 (June-Nov., 1857), pp. 164-177.

Rose, Milton C. and Emily Mason, Eds. *A Shaker Reader.* New York: Universe Books, 1977.

Shea, John G. *The American Shakers and Their Furniture - with measured drawings of Museum Classics.* New York: Van Norstrand Rheinhold, 1971.

Sprig, June. *Shaker Hands.* New York: Alfred A. Knopf, 1975.

Beloved Sister Anna, Receive this, with my never ending love and blessing, Polly Laurence. Given by Mother Lucy's permission, with a bright jewel of her love. Jan, 1855.

The drawings shown here contain much symbolism, many pious sentiments and verses. The symbols are obscure to most people today. The colors are fresh and pleasing. Most of these drawings were done between 1845 and 1859, and many were done at New Lebanon, New York and Hancock, Massachusetts.

Index